ISLAM & EDUCATION

The ISLAM &... series

Education
Technology and Science
The Politics of Power
Literature
Economics

BOARD OF EDITORS

Abdalhaqq Bewley
Uthman Ibrahim-Morrison
Aisha Bewley
Abdassamad Clarke
Dr. Tobias Sahl Andersson

Islam & Education

Edited by
Uthman Ibrahim-Morrison

Copyright © Diwan Press, 2025/1447

Islam & Education

Published by:	Diwan Press
	311 Allerton Road
	Bradford
	BD15 7HA
	UK
Website:	www.diwanpress.com
E-mail:	info@diwanpress.com

All rights reserved. No part of this publication may be reproduced, stored in any retrieval system or transmitted in any form or by any means, electronic, mechanical, photocopying, recording or otherwise without the prior permission of the publishers.

Editor-in-Chief: Uthman Ibrahim-Morrison

Authors: Shaykh Dr. Abdalqadir as-Sufi, Abdalhaqq Bewley, Uthman Ibrahim-Morrison, Imam al-Ghazālī, Dr. Amjad Hussain, Ahmad Gross, Muhammad Mukhtar Medinilla, Ibrahim Lawson, Jakob Werdelin, Abdassamad Clarke

"Ayyuhal Walad" by Imam al-Ghazali, and translated by the late David C. Reisman (1969-2011), was published in *Classical Foundations of Islamic Educational Thought* edited by Cook, Bradley J. and Malkawi, Fathi H., Brigham Young University Press, Provo Utah, 2010.

We are grateful to the Dallas Foundation for permission to reprint Shaykh Dr. Abdalqadir as-Sufi's essay: "The Collaborative Couple".

A catalogue record of this book is available from the British Library.

ISBN-13	978-1-914397-40-0	Casebound
	978-1-914397-41-7	Paperback
	978-1-914397-47-9	ePub and Kindle

Contents

Dedication	xi
The *Islam &...* Series	xiii
Root Islamic Re-education	1
Abdalhaqq Bewley	
Educating the Child	18
By Shaykh Abdalqadir	
A Cautious Welcome to the Learning Community	21
Uthman Ibrahim-Morrison	
Ayyuhal Walad (O Son!)	36
Imām al-Ghazālī	
Tarbiya	63
Dr. Amjad Hussain	
Bildung and the Return of Culture	82
Ahmad Gross	
Education and the Art of Matchmaking	96
Uthman Ibrahim-Morrison	
Islamic Education versus Assimilation	114
Muhammad Mukhtar Medinilla	
The Collaborative Couple	136
Shaykh Dr. Abdalqadir as-Sufi	
The Essentials of Classical Paideia	149
Uthman Ibrahim-Morrison	

For Whom the Bell Tolls – The Trojan Horse
Autopsy Toolkit   165
Uthman Ibrahim-Morrison, Ibrahim Lawson, Jakob
Werdelin, Abdassamad Clarke

Applying the Educational Thought of Shaykh Dr.
Abdalqadir as-Sufi   206
Muhammad Mukhtar Medinilla

بسم الله الرحمن الرحيم
وصلى الله على سيدنا محمد
وعلى آله وصحبه أجمعين وسلم

Dedication

To Shaykh Dr. Abdalqadir as-Sufi (1930-2021), the *Murabbī*, the fosterer of others' growth par excellence, educator of men, women, and children, many of whom have become in turn educators.

The *Islam &...* Series

This series deals with our world situation in all its dimensions, not just the political and economic, and the need to make sense of it and survive it. The writers have emerged from lived community life, from learning communities, in which finding answers to the issues we face is urgent, rather than a purely theoretical or academic matter.

Thus the *Islam &...* Series brings together authors who examine our situation from Muslim and non-Muslim, classical, pre- and post-modern, scientific and humanist, academic and everyday experiential standpoints that converge in startling and productive ways. They draw on the Book and the Sunna, science, the arts, philosophy and metaphysics, and history to make sense, and they summon Imam Malik, Carl Schmitt, Aisha Bewley, Malcolm X, Ibn Juzayy al-Kalbi, D. H. Lawrence, Werner Heisenberg, Wolfgang von Goethe, Martin Heidegger, Antonio Damassio, Thomas Arnold, and pre-eminently Shaykh Dr. Abdalqadir as-Sufi/Ian Dallas, as witnesses.

The range of topics in the series – education, the politics of power, technique and science, society through literature, and economics – help us to understand where we are, how we got here, where we would like to be, and how to get there, a far from abstract desire.

Root Islamic Re-education[1]
Abdalhaqq Bewley

Say: *O you who disbelieve – who cover up the truth, I do not worship what you worship, and you do not worship what I worship; I am not a worshipper of what you worship and you do not worship what I worship. You have your deen and I have my deen.* (Sūra 109)

Almost all Muslims know these words from the Qur'an by heart, and many recite them once or more every day, yet not many really reflect on their meaning or realise the importance they hold for the people of this time. It is almost as though, in the repetition of the basic premise of the *sūra*, that two kinds of worship are being highlighted. The first kind – the gross idolatry of literally turning physical forms into objects of worship – is something that all Muslims are protected from doing as long as they hold to even the most basic elements of Islam. The Prophet ﷺ said in a well known *hadith*: "By Allah, I am not afraid that you will worship others besides Allah after me, but I am afraid that you will strive and struggle against each other over these treasures of the world." To do that would be the unforgivable wrong action of open *shirk*.

However, as the Prophet ﷺ also made clear there is also such a thing as hidden *shirk*, the unconscious association of other things with Allah, and it is perhaps this that the second,

---

[1] A lecture delivered in Granada, December 2013.

repeated declaration refers to. In the *sūra* Allah commands His Messenger ﷺ to declare himself free of associating anything whatsoever with his Lord either outwardly or inwardly. But, while his community are protected from associating anything outwardly with Allah, from open *shirk*, the Muslims as a whole are certainly prone to inward association, to hidden *shirk*. Indeed Allah tells us in His Book near the end of Sūra Yūsuf: *"Most of them do not believe in Allah without associating others with Him,"* (12:106) and the Prophet ﷺ referred to it on several occasions.

The *sūra* ends: *"You have your deen and I have my deen"* making it clear that Allah's *deen* is that *deen* in which He alone is worshipped, in which nothing is associated with Him, and that this is what differentiates it from the *deen* of the unbelievers. But what exactly is the unbelievers' *deen*, what form does it take in today's world? The *hadith* of the Prophet ﷺ, *"kufr is one milla, one system of belief,"* has never been more demonstrably true than now. The dominant ethos of the world we live in is often referred to as the Judaeo-Christian tradition and, although it has in fact almost nothing to do with either Judaism or Christianity as religions, it can certainly be said to have grown out of the civilisation founded on these two religious traditions. It in fact finds its roots in the ancient world and, subverting seven centuries of enlightened input from the world of Islam while borrowing from it freely, it created a leviathan within the Judaeo-Christian world, the ongoing heir of the empire of ancient Rome, that has now overwhelmed the whole globe.

The most obvious outward manifestation of this domination is the dazzling technological superiority achieved through the scientific advances of the past few centuries that has been so crucial to the way that every aspect of human life is now conducted and controlled. What is not so readily appreciated is that this technological dominance is the direct outcome of a lengthy and deeply searched philosophical tradition, which underpins everything that has happened in the modern world. Some landmark figures in this tradition are Plato, Aristotle, Erasmus. Descartes, Hobbes, and Kant but, of course, there were many other significant thinkers betwixt and between them.

The end result of these two millennia of thought has been a very particular understanding of the human creature, which can be very loosely generalised as the increasing subjectivisation of the individual human being and the increasing objectivisation of the surrounding world. A fundamental picture of the human being was definitively formulated, which posited a basic dualism of mind/matter, spirit/body, subject/object, inner perception/outer world, and between the two there was a hard and fast division. In this definition man has become a thinking mind, stuck in a material body, looking out on an alien world of separate things outside himself.

The inevitable consequence of this was the abandonment of a traditional view of existence based on Divine Revelation, which had held sway until that time and which saw all existence as a unified whole. It was replaced by a perspective in which the mathematical science of the world and its phenomena took precedence over everything else. Descartes, who was as much a scientist as he was a philosopher, put it thus: "I perceived it to be possible to arrive at a knowledge highly useful in life ... to discover a practical, by means of which, knowing the force and action of fire, water, the stars, the heavens, and all the other bodies that surround us ... we might also apply them in the same way to all the uses to which they are adapted and thus render ourselves the lords and possessors of nature." And

Francis Bacon, another 17th Century philosopher/scientist, who is best known for his dictum that God works in Nature only by secondary causes, encapsulated this position by saying, "Those therefore, who determine not to conjecture and guess, but to find out and know – not to invent fables and romances of worlds, but to look into and dissect the nature of this real world – must consult only things themselves."

This led inexorably step by step to *Principia Mathematica*, the magnum opus of Isaac Newton, in which he formulated the laws of mechanics and gravity and which proved to be the fundamental work for the whole of modern science. In it Newton formulated what he called the law of universal gravitation and the three fundamental laws of mechanics, to the incalculable advancement of scientific knowledge, even if to the eventual detriment of the natural and human environments. There are few people who have so changed other people's perception of the universe they live in. After Newton mystery disappeared from the universe. Everything was now self-explanatory in terms of mutually dependent, internally self-consistent, interactive forces needing no extra-universal stimulus. Professor E.A. Burtt writing about what had happened says:

> "It was of the greatest consequence for succeeding thought that now the great Newton's authority was squarely behind that view of the cosmos, which saw in man a puny irrelevant spectator (insofar as a being wholly imprisoned in a dark room can be called such) of the vast mathematical system whose regular motions according to mechanical principles constituted the world of nature…"

The world that people had thought themselves living in – a world rich with colour and sound, a world of purposive harmony and creative ideals – no longer existed except in imagination. The real world outside was a hard, cold, colourless, silent and dead world – a world of quantity, a world of mathematically computable motions in mechanical regularity. In Newton, the Cartesian metaphysics found its perfect expression and finally became the predominant worldview of modern times.

The age of scientific materialism had been born.

It might be asked what all this has to do with the subject of this talk – the need for Muslim re-education – but the fact is that the worldview propagated by this philosophical tradition, culminating as we have seen in the work of Descartes and Newton, rapidly disseminated itself and soon became part and parcel of the way more and more people saw themselves and the world they lived in. It became embedded in the education systems of every part of the world and it is true to say that almost everyone is now indoctrinated in its precepts from the moment of their birth, so that there are now very few human beings indeed, Muslims included, who do not view the world in its light. The problem for Muslims is that there are unresolvable contradictions between the understanding of existence inherent in this worldview and the basic teachings of Islam. To start with there is the rigid dualism referred to earlier, the unequivocal separation of subject and object, of mind and matter, of inner perception and outer world. When this is taken to its logical conclusion it leads to a situation where a true understanding of *tawhid*, of the essential unity of existence, the absolute foundation of all Islamic teaching, becomes, intellectually speaking, virtually impossible to achieve.

Another way that an authentic understanding of *tawhid* is undermined by the scientific worldview is its rigorous reliance on causality in its methodology. Bacon started the ball rolling by definitively removing the Divine from any involvement in the physical universe with his dictum: "God works in nature only by secondary causes." This was driven home by Newton's third law of motion: "For every action there is an equal and opposite reaction." This removed the Divine from any involvement whatsoever in the natural world and has been the basis of virtually all scientific experiment and discovery ever since. The problem for Muslims is that this is absolutely at odds with the Qur'anic view of the way things happen. It is made abundantly clear in many *ayats* of Allah's Book that there is direct Divine participation in everything that occurs in the natural world and, as Shaykh Muhammad ibn al-Habib reiterated time and time again in his discourses, to attribute effects to their causes is hidden *shirk* – in other words an unconscious denial of *tawhid* – because in every instance there is no actor but Allah. The effect accompanies the cause; it is not brought about by it. Both are equally created by Allah at the moment of their occurrence.

However, as I said, scientific materialism has now intruded into every aspect of life and every corner of the earth and our education merely serves to reinforce it and articulate it. The Muslims have been subjected to this indoctrination process along with everyone else and it might be said that we are, in a way, in a worse position than non-Muslims because we think that, because we have the formulae of *tawhid* on our tongues, we are somehow immune from the insidious effects of the scientific worldview. But, in my experience, Muslims are just as susceptible to its deceptions as non-Muslims and often more so. I have talked over the last forty years to a great many Muslims about this matter and what I have found is that almost all of them have a completely Baconian approach to the subject. For them science and religion occupy separate spheres, different spaces in their consciousness.

They in fact posit the truth of science as being somehow distinct from the truth of religion. In the mosque and the Islamic students' society they use one language and in the laboratory and classroom quite another. The scientific worldview is necessarily based on Bacon's dictum that God only works in the universe through secondary causes. But the God the Muslim worships in the mosque is by definition the only Actor without intermediary in every phenomenon. These Muslims are leading double lives, often without realising it. No, there is no doubt that the Muslims' understanding of *tawhid* has been weakened and corrupted by the dominant worldview. Like almost everybody else, the modern Muslim has in fact divorced the Divine from direct involvement in natural processes, seeing them only in terms of secondary causation, and is therefore precluded from seeing things as they really are. He too views existence through a Galilean telescope and sees a Newtonian mechanistic universe with a mind permeated by Cartesian dualism.

And we should not be surprised at this since the Prophet ﷺ told us it would happen. As I said earlier the scientific worldview we have been looking at is the inevitable endgame of the Judaeo-Christian tradition. The Prophet ﷺ once said, "You will surely follow the ways of those who came before you, span by span and yard by yard, so that even if they enter into a lizard's hole you will enter it." The Companions asked, "Do you mean the Jews and Christians?" He replied, "Who else!?" And it is absolutely the case that the view of existence finally formulated by Descartes and Newton is a dark tunnel with a dead end and no exit.

However, although the Cartesian/Newtonian model seemed to be a complete description of existence and was immensely effective, in that it endowed human beings with the ability to manipulate nature to their own advantage and gave great power and profit to those with the most understanding of it – even if to the eventual extreme detriment of the planet on which they live – it has turned out to be, in fact, a very incomplete picture of even the very things it purported to be the definitive explanation of. That very matter, the solid substance upon which the whole edifice rested and of which it was supposedly built, was suddenly discovered to be quite other than had been supposed. Rather than being the lifeless substance posited by Newton, mechanistically determined by being acted on by outside forces, it turned out, at its very heart, to be composed of energy itself. Rather than being inert and predictable it was now seen to be, in reality, highly dynamic and extremely unpredictable.

In the year 1927 two things happened that were to demonstrate once and for all that the model that had held sway for three centuries, that was the bedrock on which the modern world was based, that had become the very basis of human cognition of the world, was actually a completely inadequate, even false, description of the natural world. These two things were the publication of Heisenberg's paper on his "Uncertainty Principle" and the publication of Heidegger's magnum opus *Being and Time*.

Einstein had already cast doubt on many of Newton's absolute certainties and, building on the work of his predecessors in researching the sub-atomic world, Planck and Rutherford, Werner Heisenberg, in close collaboration with his great friend and teacher, Niels Bohr, developed his "uncertainty principle". In one stroke the Newtonian description of existence was torn to shreds. This is not the time, nor am I even minimally qualified, to go into the details of the science involved, but the end result of Heisenberg's work in quantum mechanics was to show definitively that the rigid separation between the human observer and the outside world he was observing, on which all scientific experimentation was based, did not in reality exist. Fritjof Capra, himself a contemporary atomic physicist of considerable standing, expressed in a particularly lucid and eloquent way the implications of Heisenberg's research when he wrote:

> "When quantum mechanics – the theoretical foundation of atomic physics – was worked out in the 1920's, it became clear that even the sub-atomic particles were nothing like the solid objects of classical physics... At the sub-atomic level the solid material of classical physics dissolves into wave-like patterns of probabilities... A careful analysis of the process of observation in atomic physics has shown that the sub-atomic particles have no meaning as isolated entities but can only be understood as correlations between the preparation of an experiment and the subsequent measurement. This implies, however, that the Cartesian division between the I and the world cannot be made while dealing with atomic matter. Quantum mechanics thus reveals a basic oneness of the Universe. As we penetrate into matter, nature does not show us any isolated basic building blocks, but rather appears as a complicated web of relations between the various parts of the whole and these relations always include the observer in an essential way."

The rigid dualism of the Newtonian model has thus been shown to be a scientific fallacy and the existence of an underlying unity, at both the macrocosmic and microcosmic level, has been scientifically demonstrated to be the true description of the universe we inhabit. This has once more opened the way to a truly authentic understanding of *tawhid*, something acknowledged by Heisenberg himself. He was asked if he believed in a personal God and replied, "May I rephrase your question? If you are asking can you, or anyone else, reach the central order of things or events, whose existence seems beyond doubt… I would say yes." And he further said on the same occasion, "…let's hope the central realm will light our way again, perhaps in quite unsuspected ways."

What was sealed by Heisenberg in the world of the physical sciences was accomplished by Heidegger in the philosophical realm. The powerful Western philosophical tradition we earlier traced from Plato to Kant continued to remain strong throughout the 19th century but the 20th century saw it lose relevance as it petered out in a mire of abstruse and arcane linguistic abstractions. A major exception to this trend was the work of Martin Heidegger and with his publication of *Being and Time* he cut through two thousand years of philosophy to reopen, as he said, "the question of being". In doing this he redefined the understanding of what it is to be a human being. As his greatest student and fellow philosopher Hans Georg Gadamer said: "Martin Heidegger changed the philosophical consciousness of the time with one stroke… the brilliant scheme of *Being and Time* really meant a total transformation of the intellectual climate, a transformation that had lasting effects on almost all the sciences. His thinking has penetrated everywhere and works in the depths often unrecognised – but nothing today is thinkable without it."

Again I am in no way qualified to give even a resumé of Heidegger's philosophy, but suffice it to say that with Heidegger man is no longer considered as a mind in a physical body looking out on a separate world of things outside himself but as dasein – literally "being-there" – a complex fusion of past, present and future and the world he lives in. Comparing his conclusions directly with those of his friend Heisenberg in the subatomic world he said, "Microphysics must accept the impact of the instruments into the experiment when perceiving its objects. This means that the experiencing-bodiness of man is encompassed within the objectivity of the physical discovery. We must ask, 'Is this only applicable to scientific research?' ... It can only be seen as the critical overcoming of the up to now ruling of the subject/object relationship... as the fundamental character of the human dasein." In other words human beings can no longer be considered to be in any real way separate from the world that surrounds them. The Cartesian duality is actually a delusion. This once more opens the way to a genuine intellectual understanding of *tawhid* precluded by the old way of thinking. This is made absolutely clear by Heidegger in his insistence that the human being can only be truly brought to life by the search for the meaning of Being Itself, about which he says:

> "Being is what is emptiest and at the same time it is abundance, out of which all beings – known and experienced, or unknown and yet to be experienced – are endowed each with the essential form of its own individual being.
>
> "Being is most universal, encountered in every being, and is therefore most common: it has lost every distinction

or never possessed any. At the same time Being is most singular, whose uniqueness cannot be attained by any being whatsoever. Over and against every being that might stand out, there is always another just like it; that is another being, no matter how varied their forms may be. But Being itself has no counterpart.

"Being reveals itself to us in a variety of oppositions that cannot be coincidental, since even a mere listing of them points to their inner connection. Being is both utterly void and most abundant, most universal and most unique, most intelligible and most resistant to every concept, most in use and yet to come, most reliable and most abyssal, most forgotten and most remembering, most said most impossible to express."

There are few clearer or more complete expositions of pure Unicity than that contained in these few lines.

So it is undoubtedly the fact that significant breakthroughs have been made both in the scientific and philosophical fields but the problem is that their implications, although they are apparent in every sphere at the leading edge of scientific and intellectual research, have not yet even found their way into the education system let alone penetrated the level of general consciousness. This means that the discredited Cartesian/Newtonian worldview – what has become known as modernism – is still being taught as a true picture of the human being and the world we live in and is accepted as such by the vast majority of the human race.

This is particularly detrimental where the Muslims are concerned for two reasons. Firstly, as I explained earlier, the modernist perspective attacks the most fundamental aspect of

Allah's *deen*, the core teaching of Islam, a pure understanding of *tawhid*, and, as I said at the very beginning of this essay, it is precisely that which differentiates Islam from the *deen* of kufr. In the ways I pointed out, and many more that I have not, the thorough indoctrination in it that all of us have received from the day we were born makes it extremely difficult for Muslims of this time to have an authentic grasp of true *tawhid*.

The second reason is that, perhaps because they came late to the party, the Muslims were almost indecently eager to swallow the modernist perspective whole. Dazzled by European power and technological superiority, they mistakenly allowed themselves to attribute this to the backwardness of the teachings of Islam and, by wholeheartedly embracing the Western educational system, jettisoned the traditional Islamic model and undermined the very foundations on which the strength of Islam depended. Students went from Cairo, one of the great centres of Muslim education, to study "higher learning" in Paris and London. The *tanzimat* reforms, based entirely on European ideas, which included the development of a new secular school system, the reorganisation of the army based on the Prussian conscript system, the creation of provincial representative assemblies, and the introduction of new codes of commercial and criminal law, largely modelled after those of France, were implemented throughout the Ottoman Caliphate. The Muslim élite in the Indian subcontinent were put through the English education system and established institutions based on it. In the Middle East and Africa the French imposed theirs.

The failure of the Islamic movements of this time such as the Ikhwan al-Muslimeen and the Jam'at al-Islami is due to this. They all trace their roots back to the reformers al-Afghani and Muhammad Abduh, both of whom were absolutely immersed in, and in love with, the modernist worldview. It has particularly affected the better-educated strata of Muslim society. The best minds and brightest intellects of the Muslim world, which formerly would have been trained within the worldview dictated by the Qur'an and the Islamic sciences, have for well over a century now been subjected to an entirely secular modernist education. For this reason it is absolutely vital that the Muslims of today, who are mostly completely unaware of the subtle dangers of the education process they have gone through, become aware of them and go about counteracting them in every way they can. In this context the significance of an event that took place in June 1968 cannot be overstated: the meeting between Ian Dallas – soon to become Shaykh Abdalqadir as-Sufi – and Shaykh Muhammad ibn al-Habib al-Amghari al-Idrisi.

The French did not enter Morocco until 1912. By this time Shaykh Muhammad ibn al-Habib was already a middle-aged man, teaching in the Qarawiyyin in Fez. This means that he had had an absolutely traditional Muslim education, totally uninfluenced by any of the modernist trends I have mentioned. It was an education process that had been going on in Fez uninterruptedly for more than a thousand years and could be directly traced back to the Madina of Imam Malik and before him to the Prophet ﷺ and his Companions. His was the last generation of Muslims about whom this can authentically be said. In other words he was entirely untainted by the modernist worldview that has proved so corrosive to a true understanding of *tawhid*: the essential knowledge that underpins all other Islamic teachings. This shines through in his *Diwan* and in his surviving derses and is perhaps the reason why so much of his teaching emphasises, indeed insists on, the need for a pure *tawhid* and explains how it can be achieved.

Shaykh Abdalqadir, on the other hand, was someone who had been entirely educated within the modernist ethos. He had not, however, been content to remain within its imprisoning walls but had burst through them, embracing wholeheartedly the breakthroughs in science and philosophy I mentioned earlier. All the things I have outlined in this talk are taken from him, some as almost direct quotations from what he has written and others through years of reflection on what he has taught. This meant that he was an ideal person to receive from Shaykh Muhammad ibn al-Habib the pure teaching of the *deen* that had been transmitted to him from those before him. By his repudiation and transcendence of the Cartesian/Newtonian dead end maze – the modernist worldview – he was truly and authentically able to absorb and pass on a true understanding of *tawhid*. His book *The Way of Muhammad* makes clear the path he took to it and his *Book of Tawhid* is, undoubtedly, an explicit example of the purity of his understanding of it, but the truth is that all his writing and teaching is shot through, is underpinned, by his unerring knowledge of it.

Their meeting took place in the Moroccan town of Kenitra, which means in Arabic "The Bridge", and their meeting was indeed a bridge. It was a bridge that overpassed completely the three centuries of the modernist project and its deceptive half-truths about the nature of existence. The meeting between Shaykh Muhammad ibn al-Habib and Shaykh Abdalqadir as-Sufi linked traditional, unalloyed, knowledge of *tawhid*, the central and core teaching of Allah's *deen*, directly to the renewed ability to authentically understand it opened up by the recent discoveries about the true nature of matter and the human being. From the very beginning it is this and this alone that has been the driving force of Islam. It was their unequivocal belief in the limitless power of Allah, without any intermediary, that enabled the first community to conquer half the known world in a single generation; and it is this same uncompromising belief in Allah's absolute unity that has been the basis of every growth of Islam ever since. It is noteworthy that the weakness of Islam in recent times has coincided with the undermining of the integrity of this belief by the exposure of the Muslims to the doctrines of scientific materialism inherent in the modernist worldview.

What is needed now is a new growth of Islam and for this to happen it is necessary for the Muslims of this time to break out of the straitjacket of the modernist perspective in the way demonstrated by Shaykh Abdalqadir and take on again a belief in Allah that is absolutely untainted by any association whatsoever. We have to bring out a new growth of Islam from the very texture of our own time, an expression of Islam that will transcend and transform the classical tradition of Greece and the European tradition that has enmeshed the whole world but that is now, as we have seen, at a point where it is once more potentially and authentically open to Allah's *deen*, the living reality of Allah's Book and the Sunna of His Messenger ﷺ.

The Qur'an is the uncreated word of Allah, outside space and time. We must rediscover the *ayats* in the present, reflect on them anew, seek out their light and energy and make them our springboard for the re-establishment of Allah's guidance in this time. The Sunna is the archetypal record of how human perfection, in the person of the Prophet ﷺ, turned Divine Guidance into a living reality and how he and his Companions ؓ completely transformed themselves and their situation. To follow the Sunna, we must discover something of the qualities of the Prophet ﷺ in ourselves, transform ourselves in the way the Companions did, transform our situation as they did theirs. In other words, we must go forwards to the Book and Sunna, not back to them. The people of our time need Islam freshly cooked, not reheated. We must have the thing itself not an imitation. Nothing else will do.

This is certainly not a task for the faint-hearted. It will require great courage, total commitment and absolute trust in Allah. What is needed is a new generation of Muslims, who have repudiated the superficial half-truths of scientific materialism; new men and women who are ready and able to face the challenge of this new age; who are capable of transforming themselves and the society they live in; who have broken out of the enslaving enchantment of the modernist perspective with its false view of existence, its illusory shadow-show politics, and its real economic domination; who are determined to grasp the opportunities opened up by the newly emerging worldview; whose lives are devoted to establishing Allah's *deen* anew in all its justice, mercy, simplicity, splendour and power. They will truly be able to say with absolute sincerity to the unbelievers around them: *"You have your deen and I have my deen – Lakum deenukum wa liya deen."*

Educating the Child[1]
By Shaykh Abdalqadir

The education of the child centres around its first desire: FOOD.

When ready, he should be taught:
- table manners of Sunna
- begin Bismillah
- use the right hand
- eat what is near
- do not look greedily at another eating
- avoid haste in eating: Chew well
- do not take morsel in quick succession
- do not linger or play with food
- do not smear hands excessively
- do not smear clothes
- do not overeat
- modest eaters should be praised before the child
- he should be encouraged to hand over food and go without for someone else

Boys should be taught to be content with plain clothes and disdain silks.

---

1 This typewritten document served as helpful guidance to young Muslim families in Shaykh Abdalqadir's community in the '70s.

Educating the Child

He should learn Qurān and stories of Awliya[2] so that love may take root in the heart and connect him to the Unseen.

Good actions should be both rewarded and praised.

Undesirable acts should first be overlooked.

Scolding must not be frequent. Frequent scolding is ineffective and establishes the fault.

He should be discouraged from talking:

– nonsense

– obscenity

– indiscretion

If punished, it should be at the time of misbehaving and without fuss or fury. Immediately afterwards, it should be connected verbally to him with the deed (and not with the doer of the punishment) – by the other parent.

The father must talk to the child.

The mother must openly express her having the same view of Reality as the father.

The child's secrets should on no account be revealed.

The child should on no account sleep in the daytime (normally), but must have uninterrupted night sleep.

Beds should not be soft.

The child should get a walk regularly.

Taught to avoid yawning.

The child not be allowed to do anything in secret.

He should not boast of his father's possessions, nor be vain of what he eats, wears, owns.

---

2 Later the Shaykh began to discourage teaching children stories and historical material such as sira before the age of *tamyiz* – the age when children learn to discriminate between imagination and reality, since if taught too early the adult in later life would have a dreamlike fantasy-laden image of the *deen*.

Gentleness and humility are manly virtues.

He should refrain from accepting things from others.

If he is rich, he should learn to spend on others. If poor, told that accepting from others is a mark of greed.

After study there must be play or life will be bitter.

At the age of *Tamyiz* (discretion), he is taught *wudhu* and *salat*: cleanliness.

At adolescence he is initiated into the meaning of the Hidden Reality and shown the impermanence of this world.

He is ready to hear about Time.

A Cautious Welcome to the Learning Community
Uthman Ibrahim-Morrison

Preamble

The ancient roots of the august and venerable University of Cambridge, as is well known, lie in the English religious establishment, dedicated to the service of the Divine and the study of the Divinities. This is so clearly the case that historically the university suffered an enormously negative impact from the dissolution of the monasteries by Henry VIII and related political implications, which go some way to explaining the reorientation from its 'pre' – or early Renaissance character to its more recognisable post-Renaissance or Enlightenment emphasis on achieving excellence and prestige in utilitarian, scientific endeavours, humanistic intellectual studies and study of the liberal arts. I am surely not alone in my suspicion that the university's subsequent achievements would hardly have been possible without the original religious foundations which provided this proud institution with the ethical and disciplinary standards, practices and scholarly traditions in which its great reputation is rooted. Only time will tell what longer term costs and consequences will result from the all too precipitate and comprehensive abandonment of these auspicious underpinnings, in exchange for calculated returns from serving the secular-utilitarian, scientific and 'technique-driven' requirements and priorities of the industrial-enterprise nexus. Whatever the future outcome, I cannot help thinking that it will end up an unhappy bargain, and whether or not it will ever be possible to trace the chains of causation back to their roots in an empirically convincing manner will, no doubt, depend upon where questions regarding the evaluation of the matter will register on the scale of managerial and budgetary priorities – not very highly, I suspect.

However, in the unlikely event that an explanatory correlation is ever identified or even investigated, between traditional religiosity and a positive conduciveness of the scholastic environment towards intellectual excellence and high achievement, whether institutional or individual, such as to indicate the advisability of a return to earlier traditions, one would hope that the generous presence of Muslim teachers and students would instantly be recognised as an obvious means of retracing the route back, or at least, as an important reservoir of the long neglected, underestimated and increasingly scarce commodity I am calling 'traditional religiosity'. To my dismay, what we find instead on university campuses, predictably enough, is Muslim teaching and studentship being overshadowed by distracting controversies concerning radicalisation and separate seating arrangements for males and females. Is this to be the lasting contribution with which Muslims will be permanently identified? Is this to be the primary component of Muslim student identity in the British higher educational environment? If so, it does not leave us with much to look forward to when our account with history is being settled, let alone on that Day when Allah, *ta'ala*, inspects our books! (May He show us mercy!). Of course, we will not be questioned on that momentous Day about what others did in their time and situations, but it is well for us to bear in mind today the behaviour of the leading lights of the revolutionary Sokoto Jihad in West Africa[1] who, when faced with similar issues that threatened to derail the entire movement, in the form of the loud and intractable opposition from hypocritical and corrupted 'ulama who, out of self-interest, wished to preserve the status quo ante on behalf of their increasingly jittery local rulers and paymasters, to the mixed assemblies that the jihad movement's leaders had deemed appropriate in order for women to have direct access to necessary and obligatory knowledge, they ceded neither the moral, nor the intellectual, nor the political high ground to their opponents, neither did they allow themselves to be dictated to by the ignorant or differ amongst themselves in their responses, which were therefore, issued with unambiguous confidence, clarity, sincerity and unerring effectiveness. Their high training in *adab* also ensured that they were more than sufficiently well equipped to hold their own in the intellectual confrontations that were frequently conducted through the exchange of arguments composed and delivered in verse, either in Arabic or in the local Hausa and Fulfulde languages of the Fulani peoples, using a succinct and compressed metrical style and phrasing, known to be effective in penetrating hearts and minds:

[1] By the time the *khilafa* was fully established (1808-9), three leading figures had clearly distinguished themselves as the historical pillars of the new order. Firstly, Shehu Usman dan Fodio himself, regarded as the *mujaddid* in person; secondly, his brother, 'Abdullahi dan Fodio, the finest and most complete scholar the movement produced, he was also its philosopher, political and military strategist, and conscience; and thirdly, Muḥammad Bello, the Shehu's son, the energetic, trustworthy leader, destined to serve as the real architect and consolidator of the new political reality.

"The open debate on women was sparked off in Daura in 1201/1786-7 by a scholar named Mustafa Goni. It was he who, according to 'Abdullahi in *Tazyin*[2], first openly challenged the Shehu on his allowing women to attend his public lectures. In a message to the Shehu, Mustafa Goni said:

'O son of Fudi, rise to warn the ignorant,
   That perchance they may understand both religion,
and the things of this world.
   Forbid women to visit your preaching,
For the mixing of men and women is a sufficient disgrace.
   Do not do anything that contributes towards disgrace,
For Allah has not ordered vice which could cause us harm.'

The Shehu's immediate reaction was to ask 'Abdullahi to write Mustafa Goni a reply on his behalf:

'O you who have come to guide us aright
   We have heard what you have said.
Listen to what we say.
   You gave advice to the best of your ability,
But would that you had freed us from blame...
   We found the people of this country drowning in ignorance,
Shall we prevent them from understanding religion?
   It has been said, "Judgment shall be carried out
on a people according to the evil they create."

---

[2] *Tazyīn al-Waraqat* is an important contemporary chronicle written in Arabic by Shaykh 'Abdullahi describing both jihad and pre-jihad events, people and circumstances of the time.

Take this as a measure.'

"The central point in 'Abdullahi's reply is that, even if women's attendance at the Shehu's lectures were a disgrace, their being abandoned to ignorance was a greater disgrace. In the words of 'Abdullahi: 'The evil of leaving women in ignorance, not knowing what is incumbent upon them, nay, not knowing Islam at all, is greater than the evil of their mixing with men, for the first evil [ignorance] relates back to religion, which is *Iman*, Islam and good works (*Ihsan*), and the second evil [mixing] relates back to genealogy.'"[3]

Professor Sulaiman Ibraheem in *The African Caliphate*[4] goes on to discuss the Shehu's own thinking as preserved in his own contemporary writings:

"Women's attendance of open-air lectures, he seemed to say in the *Tanbih*,[5] was not his own innovation. Other great scholars, who faced similar circumstances of prevailing ignorance, had either allowed it or expressly recommended it. Among them, he said, were the shaykh, the imam, the learned scholar Sidi Ahmad ibn Sulayman who was "a great saint" and regarded as a "Junayd"[6] of his generation. And no less an authority than al-Ghazali[7] recommended the same. Even those such as Ibn 'Arafa, who were of the opinion that

---

[3] Reproduced in Sulaiman, Ibraheem, *The African Caliphate: The Life, Works and Teaching of Shaykh Usman Dan Fodio* (1754-1817) pp. 145-6. Diwan Press Ltd., 2009 Norwich,

[4] op. cit. pp. 147-9 see fn. 3

[5] *Tanbih al-Ikhwan*, an instructional text written by the Shehu during the Jihad period.

[6] See fn. 14.

[7] See fn. 11.

women should not go to lectures if it involved mixing with men, were referring to lectures dealing with knowledge that is not obligatory. In any case by "mixing" they meant actual direct contact between men and women and not occasions when they sit separately or when women sit in a separate compartment.

It is obligatory on a woman, he said in *Tanbih* and *Irshad*,[8] to acquire a full knowledge of her religious obligations such as prayer, fasting, *zakat*, hajj, as well as the more mundane matters such as trade and transactions. If her husband is not able to supply this knowledge, she is under an Islamic obligation to go out in search of it. 'If he refuses her the permission,' the Shehu stated categorically in *Irshad*, 'she should go out without his permission, and no blame is attached to her nor does she incur any sin by doing that.'

A ruler should compel husbands to make sure that their wives are educated in the same way that he should compel them to give the wives adequate maintenance. 'Indeed,' said the Shehu, 'knowledge is superior (to maintenance).'"

"He [the Shehu] lamented in *Irshad* the failure of women to demand their right to education in the same way that they would demand their right to maintenance and other basic needs. Women, like men, have been created for the sole purpose of serving Allah, which is not properly attainable without true education."

---

[8] For *Tanbih* see fn. 5. *Irshad al Ikhwan ila Ahkam Khuruj an-Niswan* an instructional text written by the Shehu during the Jihad period providing guidance on the legal position regarding women's out-of-door activities.

A learning community

The Shehu's teaching was transmitted in community, not in an institution. In that it was in line with Timbuktu society, for example, which was utterly given over to knowledge, and the original model of Madina of the first three generations. In our emulation of them, we formulated this motto.

AN ADAPTATION OF PLATO'S MOTTO

لا يَدْخُلُ فِينَا إِلَّا مَنِ اهْتَمَّ بِالْأَدَبِ وَالسِّيَرِ
وَطَلَبَ عِلْماً نَافِعاً

"Let none come among us except those who are concerned with *adab* and *siyar* and who seek beneficial knowledge."

This motto is based on that which Plato is said to have had appended above the entrance to the Academy in Athens, which is of course the ancestor of all modern education, not least the university:

ἀγεωμέτρητος μηδεὶς εἰσίτω

Ageōmétrētos mēdeìs eisítō.

"Let no one untrained in geometry enter," whose translation in Arabic is:

لاَ يَدْخُلُ هَذَا الْمَكَانَ مَنْ لاَ يُتْقِنُ الْهَنْدَسَةَ

We are, therefore, satisfied that, like Plato's motto, our own serves the same dual purpose; being at once a welcome of admission to the learning community for those to whom it is suited; and a warning of exclusion for those to whom it is not suited. We are equally mindful of and satisfied with the resonances it bears with the profound and insightful observation of the notable political theorist Carl Schmitt:

> "*Der Nihilismus ist die Trennung von Ordnung und Ortung* – Nihilism is the separation of order and location."[9]

Adab, Siyar and Beneficial Knowledge

There is little disagreement that the world is in a period of unprecedentedly rapid transition. It has been heralded as a brave new age of information. However, there is ample reason to regard these developments with deep pessimism and foreboding as the inexorable rise of information and technology proceeds at the expense of an authentic epistemology. The recovery of a correct hierarchy of knowledges and their application to the transactions of civilised living is urgently needed in order to discriminate between two ways of being in the world: the one essentially nihilistic and the other one life affirming.

The dynamic juxtaposition of the respective clusters of meaning contained in the Arabic words *adab* and *siyar* reveal what we consider to be the essential touchstones that guide our determination as a fellowship of scholars, academics, researchers and students to recover the vital connection between learning and behaviour and to create the opportunities for autonomy of thought and action that will be indispensable if the people of knowledge and understanding are to fulfil the responsibilities that await them in our time.

Adab contains the meanings of 'courtesy', 'discipline' and 'literature'. Courtesy is certainly one of the foremost requirements of the student and teacher in their meeting

---

[9] Carl Schmitt, *The Nomos of the Earth*

together, but it is equally a vital feature of any civilised society at all levels, whether it be at home in the family or out in the marketplace. It is nevertheless one of the first casualties of the modern age, or more accurately, the 'technique age', in which we live. When the barrier of courtesy is destroyed, then the road lies open to the inhumane barbarities to which we have become increasingly inured.

Discipline is an essential ingredient in any endeavour, not least in the fields of teaching, training and learning which are of primary concern to us.

Literature is of paramount importance on a number of levels. Firstly, it cultivates and transmits the relationship to language without which all knowledge and science are reduced to technical applications and exercises in pragmatism; a road leading to destinations which include 'total war', 'collateral damage' and genocidal 'final solutions', the abhorrent instances of which we see being carried out with greater and greater efficiency almost daily. Secondly, it is through literature that great authors and poets have transmitted their deep insights into the inner drives, actions and emotions of the human being, and have recognised the workings of history and new directions whose stirrings we must also assist, through literature and poetry, amid the otherwise dismal landscape of world politics.

Siyar contains meanings which encompass 'biographies', 'military campaigns' and 'histories'. These are the elements that will prevent any tendency in the study of *adab* towards becoming an arena of pure erudition limited to elevating but ineffectual 'arts and humanities', rather than being a source of real and effective insight into the dynamic forces that move and shape history; namely, an understanding of the individual with his knowledge and his 'training' confronted by his destiny and his responsibility.

The use of the term 'beneficial knowledge' is a necessary counter to the concept of academic studies for their own sake, since we have seen the transformation of the academic arena into a handmaiden of the powerful hegemonic political and economic forces of our age, whilst yet maintaining the myth of scientific objectivity and academic detachment. In truth, we do not deny that the discipline of scientific method has a place but neither will we deny its limitations or the limitations of the dialectical method, critical deconstruction and gratuitous polemic as a reliable means of epistemological advancement.

The Learning Community

The learning community from its base in its city will nurture a determination on the part of teachers and students to actively engage in the vital issues of the age and to inspire a new generation to assume the mantle of responsibility for indicating and ushering in the necessary revaluations and transformations whose historical immanence we can sense, but whose emergence is neither guaranteed nor inevitable without intentional participation.

A learning community is not simply an academic organisation or institution in the form one automatically imagines such things to take nowadays; rather, it is the natural, spontaneous and organic response to an urgent need on the part of a pioneering people (Muslims) in historically uncharted and demonstrably problematic territories (the modern, secular nation states of Europe and N. America). Therefore, we are pleased to declare our 'vision', our 'intention' and the 'holistic' ethos which informs our approach to education and the acquisition and conscientious implementation of knowledge. However, as confident and satisfied as we may be with the good fortune and fruitful yield that the learning community seems to hold in store for us, in the light of the knowledge indicated to us, once again, in Sura al-Kahf, the result is that, contrary to what has become standard organisational practice, we are not so willing to enter into the declaration of a 'mission', bearing in mind the core Qur'ānic teaching contained within the formula: *"Ma sha'Allahu la quwwata illa billah.":*

> *"Why, when you entered your garden, did you not say, 'It is as Allah wills, there is no strength but in Allah?'"*[10]

For the sake of clarity, we can declare without compunction, our 'vision', our 'intention' and our 'ethical position', but we hesitate at the declaration of a 'mission', not only because of this word's inherent presumption of autonomous 'power' but also because of the negative connotations that relate it to the infamous methodology and the political consequences of organised Christian proselytisation throughout the world, not least of all, the Muslim world. In addition to this we are ever mindful of the well-known report from the Prophet ﷺ, which warns us in no uncertain terms to be on guard against the inevitable dangers that await us in the form of the misguided precedents that are bound to influence our choices.

The Prophet Muḥammad ﷺ said:

> "You will surely follow the traits of those before you, handspan by handspan, cubit by cubit, to such extent that if they entered the burrow of a lizard, you would follow them (into it)." Someone asked, "Messenger of Allah, (are they) the Jews and the Christians?" He replied, "Who else!"[11]

---

[10] Qur'ān (Al-Kahf 18:38)
[11] Al-Bukhārī, *al-Jāmi' aṣ-Ṣaḥīḥ*, Kitāb al-I'tiṣām bi'l-Kitāb wa's-Sunna,

Our Vision

The establishment of a community/communities of learning whose participants are engaged in the advancement of Muslim scholarship, teaching and enquiry into the branches of knowledge and practice essential to the attainment of civic recovery and renewal within the lifetime of its/their founder members.

Our Inspiration and Our Educational Ethos

With respect to our determination, "to inspire a new generation to assume the mantle of responsibility for indicating and ushering in the necessary revaluations and transformations", the Noble Book of Allah *ta'ala* has provided us with a most inspiring indication from Sura al-Kahf in the description of the young men, to whose uprightness of character and nobility of aspiration He responds. He responds directly to their sincere reliance upon Him with a gift of mercy; having provided them with a miraculous form of refuge in a cave, He assures them of guidance and success in response to a prayer which, in its transcendent reality contains the secret immensity of Allah's gift: an instruction directly from Him to them, to ask of Him directly that which He, in His timeless knowledge and omnipotence, had already preordained for them, and consequently, for us also, since the inspiration for this prayer has also reached us in our current predicament, hence:

"When the young men took refuge in the cave and said, 'Our

---

chapter 14, ḥadīth 7320; Also Kitāb Aḥādīth al-Anbiyā', chapter 52, ḥadīth 3456; Muslim, *al-Musnad aṣ-Ṣaḥīḥ*, Kitāb al-'Ilm, chapter Ittibā' Sunan al-Yahūd wa'n-Naṣārā, ḥadīth 6781; Also at-Tibrīzī, *Mishkāt al-Maṣābīḥ*, Kitāb ar-Riqāq, chapter Taghayyur an-Nās, section 1, ḥadīth 5361. Also reported by al-Ḥākim in his *al-Mustadrak 'ala'ṣ-Ṣaḥīḥayn* on the authority of Ibn 'Abbās ⚬; as-Suyūṭī, *Jam' al-Jawāmi'*, Vol.6, p.19, ref. 16950

Lord, give us mercy directly from you and open the way for us to right guidance in our situation."¹²

Allah, *ta'ala*, continues:

*"We will relate their story to you with truth, they were young men (fitya) who had iman in their Lord and We increased them in guidance, We fortified their hearts when they stood up and said, 'Our Lord is the Lord of the heavens and the earth and we will not call on any god apart from Him. We would in that case have uttered an abomination. These people of ours have taken gods apart from Him. Why do they not produce a clear authority concerning them? Who could do greater wrong than someone who invents a lie against Allah? When you have separated yourselves from them and everything they worship except Allah, take refuge in the cave and your Lord will unfold His mercy to you and open the way to the best for you in your situation."*¹³

We also have the example of the young Prophet Ibrahim ﷺ:

*"They said, 'We heard a young man (fata) mentioning [our idols]. They call him Ibrahim.'"*¹⁴

The new generation we aim to inspire are the young men and women who aspire to, or already share, the characteristics, attitude and consternation of these Qur'anic exemplars. The necessary foil of environmental hostility against which their exceptional qualities are expected to stand out and to which they must respond surrounds them today in the actuality

---

¹² Qur'ān (al-Kahf 18:10)
¹³ Qur'ān (al-Kahf 18:13-16)
¹⁴ Qur'ān (al-Anbiyā' 21:60)

of the nihilistic secularism that characterises our current, predominantly technique-driven society. It is morphologically and semantically evident that the education and training of the '*fata*' is what is indicated in the word '*futuwwah*', that is, the transmission of nobility of character and excellent personal qualities, such as courage, sincerity, generosity and service, along with intelligence, *iman* and upright behaviour, as evidenced in the words and conduct of the young men in the cave and the young Ibrahim ﷺ. The quintessential expression of this education can be found in Imam al-Ghazali's[15] deservedly admired and highly instructive letter, 'Ayyuhal Walad' (O Son!) written in response to a request received in writing from an excellent young student and assistant who had sought advice and guidance regarding his own future direction in life. We include it here in its entirety as rendered in the fine translation of the late David C. Reisman (1969-2011) because, as an example of *adab* it is superior to anything we could have contrived to produce in our own words and it conveys with exemplary clarity and literary elegance a comprehensive summation of the learning community's educational ethos, purpose and manner of approach to the many beleaguered and noble minded young seekers who may wish to avail themselves of the rare opportunity such a community represents, to apply their intellectual talents in a manner and a setting that is entirely harmonious with their inward and outward aspirations as young Muslims preparing for confrontation with the vital issues of an age that has enthroned information and technique at the expense of

---

[15] Abū Ḥāmid Muḥammad ibn Muḥammad al-Ghazālī (1058/450-1111/505), renowned *faqīh*, philosopher and Sūfi. Known as the 'Proof of Islam'. Author of the magisterial and highly influential *Iḥyā' 'ulūm al-dīn* (Revival of the Religious Sciences).

beneficial knowledge and the cultivated good conduct they will have been taught to emulate since childhood; a confrontation bearing its own particular challenges and dangers, as indicated once more in the illuminating *ayat*s of Sura al-Kahf:

> *"Send one of your number into the city with this silver you have, so he can see which food is purest and bring you some of it to eat. But he should go about with caution so that no one is aware of you, for if they find out about you they will stone you or make you revert to their religion and then you will never have success."*[16]

---

[16] Qur'ān [Al-Kahf:19-20]

Ayyuhal Walad (O Son!)[17]
Imām al-Ghazālī[18]
(may Allah provide us benefit through it!)
In the name of Allah, the Merciful and Compassionate

(1) Praise be to Allah, Lord of the Worlds, the Final Reward of the godfearing! And blessings and peace be upon His Prophet Muḥammad and all his family!

(2) Know that a student in search of [spiritual] profit was regularly in the service of the Master and Imam, Ornament of the community and religion, the Proof of Islam, Abū Ḥāmid Muḥammad ibn Muḥammad al-Ghazālī (may Allah have mercy on him!), and devoted himself to verifying and reading [the books of] knowledge to [his master], until he had gathered together the particular details of the sciences and perfected the virtues of his soul.

(3) Then one day he was reflecting on his condition and he thought to himself: "I have read the various types of sciences and spent the prime of my life learning and harmonising them. Now I need to know which of them will benefit me in the future, bringing me solace in the tomb, and which will not, so that I might turn my back on it – as the Prophet ﷺ said:

---

[17] *Classical Foundations of Islamic Educational Thought* **edited by Cook, Bradley J. and Malkawi, Fathi H., Brigham Young University Press, Provo Utah, 2010 pp.88-107 .

[18] See footnote 15.

'Lord I seek protection in You against any useless knowledge.'" This thought stayed with him until he wrote to the honourable Master, the Proof of Islam, Muḥammad al-Ghazālī (may Allah have mercy on him!) in search of a formal opinion, asking him with certain questions and calling upon him for advice and for a prayer of supplication.

(4) He said [in his letter]: "Even though the books of the Master, such as the *Revival [of the Religious Sciences]* and others, may contain the answer to my questions, my hope is that the Master will write out my request on pages that I might keep with me throughout my life and that would survive my death, while I put into action what they contain in the course of my life, Allah willing."

(5) So the Master wrote this treatise as his response:

In the name of Allah, the Merciful and Compassionate

(6) O Son and dear friend! May Allah lengthen your days of continued obedience to Him and guide you to the path of those He loves. Know that the advice commonly available is written down from the Source of Prophecy (peace be upon him!). If any advice has reached you from him, then what need could you have for mine? And if it has not, then tell me, what have you achieved in these past years?

(7) O Son! The advice which the Messenger of Allah (blessings and peace upon him!) gave his community includes his statement:

> "One sign that Allah has turned away from His servant is [the servant's] preoccupation with anything that does not concern him. For any man who has spent so much as an hour of his life in anything unsuited to him deserves to long regret it, and anyone who has passed the age of forty

and whose good works do not outweigh his bad, let him prepare for the fire."

This is advice enough for the knowledgeable.

(8) O Son! Giving advice is easy; the problem lies in taking it, because it can taste bitter to those who follow their passions, since illicit things are in their hearts. This is especially true of anyone who pursues theoretical knowledge while being preoccupied with the soul's incitement and to worldly values, for he assumes that pure knowledge is a tool of his salvation and deliverance, and that he need not put it into practice. This is the opinion of the philosophers. Praise be to Allah, the Almighty! A fool such as this does not know that when he acquires knowledge but does not put it into practice, the judgment against him is all the stronger—as the Prophet (blessings and peace upon him!) said: "The one who will suffer most on the Day of Resurrection is the one who has knowledge which Allah renders useless to him."

(9) It was reported that Junayd[19] (may Allah sanctify his dear soul!) appeared in a dream after his death, and [the one dreaming] asked him: "What news Abū l-Qāsim?"

(10) [Junayd responded]: "Explanations miss the mark and pointers come to nought. Nothing is of use to us [in the afterlife] but the prostrations we performed in the dead of night."

(11) O Son! Do not be bankrupt in actions, nor empty-handed in the states [of your soul]. You may be certain that theoretical knowledge will not stand you in good stead. For example, if a man in the wilderness had ten swords of Indian steel and yet more weapons, and he was a man of courage, experienced in

---

[19] Abū l-Qāsim Junayd (d. 298/910) was the master of the Sufis in Baghdad in the 3rd/9th century.

battle, and if a ferocious lion leapt upon him, what say you? Would the weapons repel the menace from him without his using them and striking with them? It is common sense that they would not without his moving and striking with them. Likewise, if a man were to read a hundred thousand topics of science that he learned and studied and did not put into practice, they would be of no use to him except through action. For example, if a man had a fever or cholera, the cure for which is oxymel and barley water, recovery would not happen without using them.

(12) A poem:

Even if you pour out two thousand *ratl*s of wine,
    If you do not drink it, you are not drunk

(13) Even if you had read in the sciences for a hundred years and summarised a thousand books, you would not have prepared for the mercy [of Allah] but through action. As Allah said: "[*In the judgment of Allah] there is nought for man but his labours,*"[20] and "*whosoever hopes to meet Allah, let him do good works,*"[21] and the "*[the houris of Paradise] will be recompense for what they have done,*"[22] and "*those that believe and do good deeds shall have the gardens of Paradise as their abode,*"[23] and "*those that repent and believe and do what is right [shall be admitted to Paradise].*"[24]

(14) And what do you say to this report from the Prophet: "Islam is built upon five [principles]: the testimony that there is no god but Allah and that Muḥammad is His prophet, the performance

---

[20] Qur'ān [An-Najm 53:3]
[21] Qur'ān [Al-Kahf 18:105]
[22] Qur'ān [Al-Wāqi'ah 56:25]
[23] Qur'ān [Al-Kahf 18:102]
[24] Qur'ān [Maryam 19:60]

of the prayer, the giving of *zakāt*, the fast of Ramaḍān, and the pilgrimage to the House for those who are able."

(15) Faith is a spoken declaration, affirmation in the heart, performance of the basic requirements [of Islam], and proof of innumerable deeds. If the servant reaches Paradise through the bounty and munificence of Allah, that nonetheless comes only after he prepares himself through his obedience and worship, because *"the mercy of Allah is within reach of the ones who do good deeds."*[25] If someone were to say that [the believer] will reach Paradise through faith alone, we would say: "Yes, but when? How many precipitous paths await him before he arrives? The first of these is faith. Will he avoid being plundered and thus arriving empty-handed and destitute?"

(16) Al-Ḥasan [al-Baṣrī][26] said:

> "On the Day of Resurrection Allah will say to His servants: 'enter the Garden by My mercy and divide it among yourselves according to your deeds.'"

(17) O Son! So long as you do not act, you will not be rewarded. It is told that a man of the Israelites worshipped Allah for seventy years, and then Allah designed to display him to the angels. So He sent to him an angel to tell him that despite his worship he remained unworthy [of Paradise]. When he heard this the servant said: "We were created to worship Allah, so we should [continue to] worship Him." When the angel returned, he said, "Oh, Allah, You know better what he said." And Allah said, "Since he did not abandon worshipping Us, We in Our

---

[25] Qur'ān [Al-A'rāf 7:55]

[26] Ḥasan al-Baṣrī (d. 110/728) is one of those pivotal figures in early Islam to whom is traced so many of the later intellectual and spiritual currents.

beneficence will not abandon him. Bear witness, O angels, that I have pardoned his sins."

(18) The Prophet (blessings and peace upon him!) said:

"Judge yourselves before you are judged; take measure of yourselves before you are measured."

(19) 'Alī [ibn Abī Ṭālib] said:

"The one who assumed he fell short in his efforts will reach [the afterlife] and be granted mercy, but the one who assumed he expended every effort will arrive and find himself challenged."

(20) Al-Ḥasan al-Baṣrī (Allah have mercy on him!) said:

"Expecting Paradise without having worked [for it] is one of the sins."

(21) And he said:

"To know the true sense [of worship] is to stop thinking about the deed, but not to stop doing it."

(22) The Prophet (blessings and peace upon him!) said: "The wise man constrains himself and works towards the afterlife; the fool indulges his appetites and pursues his desires in spite of Allah.

(23) O Son! How many nights have you spent drilling yourself in knowledge and poring over books and denying yourself sleep? I do not know what is the motivation. If it is to gain worldly goods, to attract worldly ephemera, to acquire worldly appointments and compete with your peers and colleagues, then woe on you, and your judgement [in the hereafter]: woe on you! But if your aim in this is to reinvigorate the Prophet's law

(blessings and peace upon him!), to rectify your moral principles, and to break the domination of your soul, then blessings upon you, and [in the hereafter]: blessings upon you! He spoke truly, the one who said:

> Sleepless attention [to meet] another's standard makes for a wretch,
> Crying over another's loss makes a hypocrite

(24) O Son! Live your life as you see fit, for you will surely die. Desire what you want for you will surely depart. Do what you want, for you will surely pay for it. Gather up what you want, for you will surely leave it behind.

(25) O Son! What have you gained from studying theology, legal disputation, medicine, quotation books,[27] poetry, astrology, prosody, grammar and morphology but a waste of your life? By Allah the Glorious! I have seen in the Gospel of Jesus (peace upon him!) that he said:

> "From the time that the deceased is readied for his funeral until he is placed at the lip of his grave, Allah, in His glory asks him forty questions. In the first He says: 'My servant you have appeared pure to your fellowman for years, but not to me for a single hour. Every day I look into your heart and say: 'Do you not work for everyone but Me, though you be surrounded by *My* bounty?! Are you not deaf? Do you not hear?'"

(26) O Son! Knowledge without action is sheer folly, but there is no action without knowledge. Know that any type of

---

[27] *Dīwān* in the sense of a collection of of religious and historical reports, philological explanations of the Qur'ān, and sundry other material.

learning that does not distance you from sins and bring you back to obedience today will never remove you from the fire of hell tomorrow. When you do not act today, nor right your actions of past days, you will say tomorrow, on the Day of Resurrection: "Send us back to do good deeds!" and you will be told: "Oh, fool! You come now from there!"

(27) O Son! Put fervour in your spirit, resolution in your soul, and [the thought of] death in your body because your final resting place will be the cemetery, and those in their graves await you with every passing moment. Take care! Oh, take care not to arrive without provisions! Abū Bakr al-Ṣiddīq (Allah be satisfied with him!) said:

"These bodies are a cage for birds or a stable for beasts of burden. Consider, which are you? If you are a high-flying bird, then when you hear the roll of drums, return, flying up until you come to rest on the highest tower of Paradise, as [the Prophet] (peace upon him!) said: 'The throne of the Merciful rocked back and forward upon the death of Sa'd ibn Mu'ādh.'[28] But Allah protect you if you are a beast of burden! As [Allah] said: 'Those are like cattle – indeed even more misguided; those are the careless.'[29] So do not feel so certain that you will not go from the asylum of Heaven to the abyss of Hell!"

(28) It is reported that al-Ḥasan al-Baṣrī (Allah be satisfied with him!) was offered a drink of cool water, and when he took the cup he swooned and it fell from his hand. When he regained

---

[28] The chief of one of the most important tribal clans in Madinah and a supporter of the Prophet, he died shortly after the siege of Madinah in 5/627.

[29] Qur'ān [Al-A'rāf 7:179]

consciousness, he was asked: "What ails you, Abū Saʿīd?" He responded: "I thought of the yearning of those in Hell when they ask those in Paradise to *'send down some water or anything else that Allah has provided you,'* and are told that Allah has forbidden both to those who disbelieved."

(29) O Son! If theoretical knowledge is enough for you and you have no need for action in addition, then would not [Allah's] summons, "Is there someone who asks? Is there someone seeking forgiveness? I forgive him. Is there someone repenting? I excuse him," be pointless and without benefit? It is reported that a group of Companions (Allah be satisfied with them all!) mentioned ʿAbdullāh ibn ʿUmar in the presence of the Prophet (blessings and peace upon him!), who then said:

> "What an excellent man he would be if only he would pray at night!"

And [the Prophet] (peace upon him!) said to one of his companions:

> "Oh, you! Do not sleep overmuch at night; for too much sleep at night makes one a pauper on the Day of Resurrection!"

(30) O Son! *"And pray during the night"*[30] is a command. And *"[the righteous] pray at dawn for Allah's forgiveness"*[31] is a thanksgiving. And *"those who ask Allah's forgiveness at dawn"*[32] is a remembrance. He {peace be upon him!) said:

---

[30] Qurʾān [Al-Isrāʾ 17:79]
[31] Qurʾān [Adh-Dhāriyāt 51:18]
[32] Qurʾān [Āl ʿImrān 3:17]

"There are three voices that Allah loves: the voice of the rooster, the voice of the Qur'ān reciter, and the voices of those who seek Allah's forgiveness at dawn."

(31) Sufyān al-Thawrī[33] (may Allah be satisfied with him!) said:

"God causes the dawn wind to blow, carrying pious remembrances and appeals for forgiveness to Him, the King, the Almighty.' He also said: 'When someone calls out at the beginning of the night from under the throne [of Allah], 'Will not the believers arise?' they rise up and pray as long as Allah wills. Then [when he] calls out in the middle of the night, 'Will not the pious arise?' they rise up and pray until dawn. When he calls out at dawn, 'Will not the repentant arise?' they rise up, seeking forgiveness. And when he calls out at daybreak 'Will not the negligent arise?' they rise up from their beds like the dead scattering from their graves."

(32) O Son! It is reported in the counsels of Luqmān[34] the Wise to his son that he said: "'O my son! Do not let the rooster be more clever than yourself by crowing at dawn while you sleep on!" He certainly spoke well, the one who said:

Surely the pigeon in the tree had cooed
   In the thick of night, while I slumbered on.
I lied [when I swore], 'By Allah's house! If I really love [Him]
   The pigeons will not cry before me!'
I maintain that I am mad in love, possessed of passion for my Lord

---

[33] This is the Kūfan expert in Qur'ān and hadīth who died in 611/778.
[34] The figure of the sage in Islamic tradition.

> But I do not cry when the beasts do!

(33) O Son! The sum total of learning is to know the meaning of obedience and service [to Allah].

(34) Know that to obey and serve is to follow in word and deed the commands and prohibitions of the Law-Giver. This means that everything you say and do and forswear in word and deed is guided by the Law, just as though were you to fast on the 'Īd al-Aḍḥā and the last three days of the Ḥajj (the *ayyām al-tashrīq*) you would be disobedient, or were you to pray in a stolen robe, albeit the outward form [of your prayers] would be worship, you would nonetheless have sinned.

(35) O Son! Your words and actions should be in accordance with the Law, since knowing and acting without observing the Law is to go astray and become lost. You should not let yourself be dazzled by the ecstatic locutions and outcries of the Sufis, because following this path [that I outline here] requires you to strive, to cut short the passions of the soul and to slay its whims with the sword of discipline; [it is not earned] with pointless outcries and vain statements. Know that the unrestrained tongue and the heart engulfed and filled with negligence and desire are marks of misery, so much so that unless you kill your soul by means of earnest endeavour, you will never revive your heart through the light of knowledge.

(36) Know that some of the questions which you asked me cannot be given a proper response in writing or speech. In fact, if you have already reached that state, then you know well what it is. Otherwise it cannot be understood; for it is a question of experience, and no experience can be adequately described in words. The sweetness or bitterness of something cannot be known but through the experience of taste. [This is like] the

story of the impotent man who wrote to a friend: "Tell me about the pleasure of sex." And the friend wrote in response: "Oh, you! I thought you were merely impotent; now I know that you are also a fool! This pleasure is a question of experience. If you get it, you know; if not, it cannot be described by speaking or writing [about it]."

(37) O Son! Some of your questions are like this. Others can be given a proper response. In fact, we have discussed [these issues] in *The Revival of the Religious Sciences* and elsewhere, but we will recount here some selections, directing attention to them by saying: First of all, a sound belief contains no innovation. Second, you do not slip up after sincerely repenting. Third, [you should] seek reconciliation with your opponents so that none any longer has just cause against you. Fourth, [you should] acquire knowledge of the Divine Law in such a measure that you will be led to the commandments of Allah. Then [you should be acquiring] any other knowledge that [may provide you] with redemption.

(38) It is recounted that after al-Shiblī[35] (may Allah be pleased with him!) had served four hundred masters, he said: "I read four thousand reports of the Prophet, then selected one to put into practice and let the others go, because once I had reflected on it, I found that it contained my ultimate goal and salvation and that arrayed in it was the knowledge of all the early and later [believers], so it was sufficient for me. It is this: The Prophet (peace upon him!) said to one of his companions:

---

[35] This is Abū Bakr Dulaf ibn Jahdar (d. 334/945), the "sober" mystic who rebuked Junayd for the excesses of his Sufism and who denounced the mystic Hallāj during the latter's heresy trial.

'Do as much in your world as befits your station in it; do as much for your afterlife as befits the time you [hope to] remain there; do as much for Allah as befits your need for Him; and do as much for the fire of Hell as befits your ability to endure it.'"

(39) O Son! Once you act upon this report from the Prophet ﷺ, you will no longer have need for so much learning. Consider another story, Ḥātim al-Aṣamm was a friend of Shaqīq al-Balkhī.[36] [Shaqīq] asked him one day: "You have kept me company for thirty years; what have you acquired in that time?" [Ḥātim] said: "I have acquired eight lessons in knowledge, and they are enough for me, because with them I look forward to my ultimate goal and salvation." Shaqīq said: "What are they?" And Ḥātim al-Aṣamm responded: "The first lesson is that I observed mankind and saw that every person has a beloved whom he loves and desires. Some of those beloved ones accompany him to the final illness, and some to the lip of the grave, but then all return and leave him alone; none enter with him into his grave. So I thought to myself and said: 'The best beloved of man is whatever will join him in his grave and give him comfort there.' And I found that [that] is good deeds alone, so I took them into my house as my beloved so that they might be a light in my grave, keeping me comfort, not leaving me alone.

(40) "The second lesson is that I saw that people worship their caprices and leap up to serve their soul's desires. So I reflected on Allah's word: *'He who fears to stand before his Lord*

---

[36] Abū 'Alī Shaqīq ibn Ibrāhīm al-Azdī (d.193/809) was a Khurasanian mystic recognised by the later Sufi tradition as an early expert on *tawakkul* (complete dependence on Allah). Ḥātim al-Aṣamm was his foremost disciple.

and who denies his soul its whims shall have his refuge in Paradise,[37] and I became convinced that the Qur'ān is true and sincere. I would regularly leap up to oppose my soul and hasten to fight it and refuse to cede to its whims until it had been curbed and trained to obey Allah.

(41) "The third lesson is that I saw everyone trying to gather up their ephemeral gains and then hold them back in tight fists. So I reflected on Allah's word: *'What you have will dwindle away, while what Allah has will last forever,'*[38] and then I gave away my earnings and distributed it to the poor so that it might be stored up for me with Allah.

(42) "The fourth lesson is that I saw that some people believe that their prestige and eminence lie in the large number of their relatives and kin, and they let themselves be dazzled by that, while others put stock in their great amount of wealth and children, and boast about that. According to some, eminence and prestige lie in extorting, oppressing, and slaughtering people, while another group believes that [eminence and prestige] lie in merging, dispersing, and distributing wealth. So I reflected on Allah's word, *'The noblest of you in Allah's judgement is the most devout,'*[39] and I chose piety and determined that the Qur'ān is true and correct and all their convictions and beliefs utterly false.

(43) "The fifth lesson is that I saw people slandering and maligning one another, and I found the root of that to be envy over money, rank and knowledge. So I reflected on Allah's word, *'It is We who portion out to them their livelihood in this world,'*[40] and I knew that this apportionment was the pre-eternal

---

[37] Qur'ān [An-Nāzi'āt 79:39-40]
[38] Qur'ān [An-Nahl 16:96]
[39] Qur'ān [Al-Hujurāt 49:13]
[40] Qur'ān [Az-Zukhruf 43:31]

determination of Allah. So I did not envy anyone, satisfied as I was with Allah's distribution.

(44) "The sixth lesson is that I saw people feuding with one another for one reason or another. So I reflected on Allah's word, *'Satan is your enemy, so treat him as an enemy,'*[41] and I knew that fighting with anyone but Satan was unacceptable.

(45) "The seventh lesson is that I saw everyone striving assiduously and struggling excessively in pursuit of sustenance and livelihood, so much so that they would err and transgress [against the Law], debase themselves, and demean their worth. So I reflected on Allah's word, *'Allah provides for every single creature on earth,'*[42] and I knew that Allah had vouchsafed for me my sustenance. Then I turned my attention to worshipping [Him] and stopped depending on anyone else.

(46) "The eighth lesson is that I saw everyone relying on something created, whether it be money, or possessions and property, or vocations and skills, or some such created thing. So I reflected on Allah's word, *'The one who relies on God completely knows that Allah attains His purpose; Allah has measured out the worth of everything,'*[43] and I put all of my trust in Allah. He is sufficient for me – what an excellent trustee!"

(47) Shaqīq said:

> "Allah grant you success! I have pored over the Torah, the Gospel, the Psalms, and the Qur'ān and found that all four books revolve around these eight lessons. Whoever puts into practice these lessons puts into practice these books."

(48) O Son! You have learned from these two narratives that

---

[41] Qur'ān [Al-Fāṭir 35:6]
[42] Qur'ān [Hūd 11:6]
[43] Qur'ān [At-Ṭalāq 65:3]

you do not need to increase your knowledge. Now I will explain to you what is required of the traveller in search of truth.

(49) Know that the traveller must have a master, a guide, a teacher to drive out his evil dispositions and replace them with good. Educating is akin to what the farmer does when he uproots the thorn bushes, and weeds out the course plants from around the crops to ensure that they will grow well and reach their fruition. The traveller must have a master to educate him and guide him to the path of Allah. A prerequisite of the master who is worthy to serve as the Prophet's proxy is that he be learned; but not just any learned person is worthy. Let me explain to you in a summary fashion some of [such a teacher's] characteristics, lest just anyone persuade [you] that he is a guide.

(50) Anyone who relinquishes love of this world and worldly status, having followed a wise master whose spiritual descent stretches back unbroken to the most eminent of creation, the Prophet (peace be upon him!), and who has trained his soul well through little food, speech, and sleep, and much prayer, almsgiving, and fasting, and who then, by following that wise master, has fashioned from his refined virtues a particular path of patience, thanksgiving, trust in Allah, conviction, generosity, contentment, serenity, astuteness, modesty, learning, honesty, reserve, fidelity, sobriety, sedateness, deliberation and other such qualities, then he is one of the Prophet's lights and worthy of emulation. However, such a one is rare, and more magnificent than gold. The one whose good fortune leads him to find and accept the master we describe should accord him due honour outwardly and inwardly.

(51) To honour him outwardly means to neither contest him nor distract him by arguing with him over any issue, even if [you] know he is wrong. It [means] not putting his prayer rug

before him except at the call to prayer, and when he is finished, removing it. [It means] not overdoing the supererogatory prayers in his presence. [It means] doing what he orders competently and obediently. To honour him inwardly means that everything [you] hear and accept from him externally [you] do not question inwardly, whether in deed or word, lest [you] be branded a hypocrite. If [you] cannot do this, leave his company, lest what [you] think comes to conform with what [you] do. [It means] guarding against the company of the wicked in order to drain the power of satanic jinn and men from the bowl of [your] heart, that it may be washed of malevolent pollution. [It means] that in every instance poverty is to be preferred over wealth.

(52) Next, know that being a Sufi requires two characteristics: rectitude and forbearance with people. The one who seeks to be upright and virtuous with people and treats them with equanimity is a Sufi. Being upright is to sacrifice one's portion for someone else. Being virtuous with people [means] not imposing your wants upon others but rather imposing their wants upon yourself – as long as they do not contradict the Law.

(53) Then you asked me about how to serve Allah. There are three things. The first is to uphold the Law. The second is to be satisfied with the divine foreordination, decree and apportionment. The third is to trust in Allah completely, which means that your belief in what Allah has promised is firmly grounded; in other words, you believe that what He has foreordained for you will assuredly come to you, even if anyone in the world were to try to divert it from you, and that whatever was not decreed for you, you will never obtain, even if the whole world were to aid you.

(54) You also asked me about sincere devotion to Allah.

It is that all of your deeds are done for Allah and that your heart is not satisfied with what people deem praiseworthy or reprehensible. Know that hypocrisy is born of glorifying people and the cure for it is to see them as laughably incapable, to judge them to be like inanimate objects in their lack of ability to attain to either contentment or misery, so that you may rid yourself of their hypocrisies. If you judge them to be possessed of power and will, hypocrisy will never be far from you.

(55) O Son! Some of your remaining questions are treated in my writings, so look [for the answers] there. Others it is unlawful to write. Do what you know so that what you do not know may become clear to you.

(56) O Son! In the future, do not ask me about what is obscure to you but through your heart, because Allah says:

> *"If they had waited until you went out to them, it would have been better for them."*[44]

(57) Take the advice of Khiḍr[45] (peace upon him!): *"Do not ask me about anything until I myself mention it to you."*[46] Do not be impatient for [your questions] to be answered. Have you not seen [Allah's word]: *"You will soon see My signs, so be not impatient."*?[47] Do not ask before the appropriate time, and be certain that it is by the right paths that you arrive, for Allah said: *"Did they not travel the land and see the end of those who came before them?"*[48]

(58) O Son! By Allah, if you journey, you will see the wonders at every station. Expend your spirit; for the beginning [of this

---

[44] Qur'ān [Al-Ḥujurāt 49:5]
[45] In the Sufi tradition the Qur'anic figure of Khiḍr or Khaḍir represents the spiritual guide par excellence.
[46] Qur'ān [Al-Kahf 18:69]
[47] Qur'ān [Al-Anbiyā 21:37]
[48] Qur'ān [Yūsuf 12:109]

journey] is the surrender of the spirit, as Dhū al-Nūn al-Miṣrī[49] (Allah have mercy on him!) said to one of his students: "If you are able to surrender your spirit, then off we go! Otherwise do not bother yourself with the barren deserts of the Ṣūfis!"

(59) O Son! I will advise you of eight things. Accept them lest your deeds turn against you on the Day of Resurrection. Four you must do and four avoid.

(60) Among those to avoid, the first is that you do not dispute with anyone on just any issue you are able, because there is much harm and a greater sin than benefit in that, since it is the source of all reprehensible qualities such as hypocrisy, envy, haughtiness, resentment, enmity, pride, and so on. In fact, if a question came up between you and an individual or group and you wanted the truth to be set forth and not missed, then discussion would be permissible, but two conditions are required: first, that it makes no difference whether the truth be explained by you or someone else; and second, that private discussion be more preferable to you than public discussion.

(61) Listen, and I will give you a useful pointer here. Know that asking about intricate problems evinces a sickness in the heart to the doctor, and the response is to try to remedy the illness. Know that the ignorant are the ones sick at heart and the learned are the doctors. The scholar lacking in knowledge does not administer cures well, and the consummate scholar does not cure just every sick person; rather he cures only someone whom he hopes will be receptive to the cure and remedy. When the root cause is chronic or fatal, the cure will be ineffectual, so the acumen of the doctor then lies in saying

---

[49] Abū al-Fayḍ Thawbān ibn Ibrāhīm, known as Dhū al-Nūn al-Miṣrī, was an early Egyptian Ṣūfi whose name is associated with alchemy and the supernatural.

that this is unresponsive to the remedy, so there is no point to administering medicines because that would be a waste of [the patient's remaining] life.

(62) Next, know that there are four types of illness due to ignorance, one alone is receptive to cure, the remainder incurable. The first incurable illness [is that of] someone whose questioning and challenging comes from his envy and hatred. The better, more clear, and more understandable the response he is given, the more enraged and resentful he becomes. The solution, then, is not to bother to respond, [as in the line of] poetry:

> *You may hope to dispel all enmity*
> *Excepting that of the one who hates you out of envy.*

You should turn away and leave him with his disease. Allah says:

> *"Pay no heed to someone who ignores what We say and who wants only the life of this world."*[50]

The one who is envious in all he says and does kindles a fire in the field of his deeds, as the Prophet (peace be upon him!) said:

> "Envy devours the good the way fire eats through wood."

(63) The second [type of illness due to ignorance] has its root cause in stupidity, and it also cannot be treated, as ʿĪsā (peace upon him!) said:

> "Even though I managed to raise the dead, I have never been able to cure an idiot!"

---

[50] Qurʾān [An-Najm 53:28]

(64) [The idiot] is someone who devotes himself to learning for a brief time and studies a little of the rational and religious sciences and then questions and contends, not knowing anything but what is difficult for him is also difficult for the great scholar. Whenever he does not take the time to reflect in this way, his questioning and challenging being the result of idiocy, one should not bother responding to him.

(65) The third [type of illness due to ignorance is that of] someone seeking guidance who, whenever he does not understand the words of the great leaders, lays the blame on his inability to understand. Although he asks in search of aid, he is too stupid to grasp the truths. One should not bother responding to him either, as the Prophet (peace be upon him!) said:

> "We, the companies of Prophets, are commanded to address people according to their level of understanding."

(66) As for the patient [sick with ignorance] who *is* receptive to cure, he is the one seeking guidance who is intelligent, who is not overcome with envy, anger, or the love of his desires and rank and money. He is searching for the righteous path, and his questioning and contention is not out of envy, or to annoy and try one. This one is receptive to cure, so you may take the time to respond to his question – in fact, you must.

(67) The second thing you should avoid: Guard against being a preacher and semonizer, because there is much harm in that unless you first do what you say, and only then preach it to people. Reflect on what was said to 'Īsā' bnu Maryam (peace upon him!):

> "Admonish yourself, and if you take the warning, then admonish the people; otherwise, be ashamed before your Lord!"

(68) If you have been put to the test in this work, then guard against two typical characteristics [of preaching]. The first is thoughtlessly repeating moral lessons, admonitions, Qur'ānic verses and stanzas of poetry, because Allah loathes blind followers. The blind follower is the one who disregards the limit, signalling [his] interior barrenness and the negligence of [his] heart. The intention of recollecting is that the believer recall to himself the fire of the hereafter, constrain himself to the service of the Creator, reflect on his past life which consumed him with irrelevant things, reflect on the obstacles to the safety of faith that are before him at the end, and how he will be in the grasp of the King of death – will he be able to answer Munkar and Nakīr?[51] – and concern himself with his condition on the Day of Resurrection and its stages – will he cross the bridge safely or will he plunge into the abyss?[52] – and constantly recall these things in his heart so that it rouses him from his complacency. Fanning these flames and bewailing these calamities is called reminding and informing and telling people about these things and alerting them to their shortcomings and excesses and making them see their sins so that the assembly of people may sense the burning heat of these flames and grow anxious at those calamities and so that they may remind one another of their past deeds as best they can and become distressed at [the thought of] spending [their] remaining days disobeying Allah.

(69) This is the summary account of the path called preaching. It is as though you saw that a flood had swept down upon a house with the inhabitants inside and you [wanted] to say: "Beware! Beware! Flee from the path of the flood!" Would you

---

[51] The two angels who interrogate the dead in their graves.
[52] Believers must pass over a bridge between heaven and hell; those whose faith is sound will pass safely; unbelievers will plunge into hell.

in such circumstances really want to tell the owner of the house your news in hackneyed clichés, tired apothegms, and quick tips? No, you would not! That is the condition of the preacher. He should avoid it.

(70) The second characteristic [of preaching to guard against] is that it not be the goal of your sermon that the congregation bellow back their responses, exhibit excessive emotions, and rend their clothing in hysteria simply in order that it be said: "What a great assembly that was!" All of this leads to hypocrisy, born as it is of carelessness. Rather, your intention and aim should be to call people's attention away from this world to the next, from rebelliousness to compliance, from over-indulgence to temperance, from stinginess to charity, from vanity to godliness. [Your intention should be] to extol the benefits that will accrue to them in the next world, to decry this world, and to teach them how to be worshipful and abstemious, because the dominating desire in their natures is to depart from the sure path of the Law, randomly to pursue things that displease Allah, and to divert themselves immorally. So strike terror into their hearts, startle them, and warn them against the horrors they otherwise might face in the next world. And maybe their inner traits will change, their outward treatment of one another will alter, and the desire and wish to be obedient and give up rebelliousness will manifest itself.

(71) This is the way to preach and give advice. Any form of preaching that is not like this is a curse on the speaker and the listener. In fact, it is said to be a ghoul and a satan which leads people off the road and then destroys them. They must flee from it because not even Satan could do the damage to their piety that such a one [who preaches like this] would do. Anyone with the strength and will must drag [such a preacher] down from the minbars of the believers and prevent him from his

pursuit, for [such an act] is part of commanding the right and forbidding the wrong.

(72) The third thing you should avoid: Neither associate with princes and kings nor even express an opinion about them, for thinking about them, attending their courts, and associating with them is very dangerous. If you have been tempted [to do this], immediately stop both censuring and praising them, because Allah grows angry when one praises the sinner and tyrant. Anyone who has prayed for the long life [of a ruler] has clearly deemed it acceptable to rebel against Allah in His world.

(73) The fourth thing to avoid: Do not accept presents and gifts from rulers, even if you know [that the gifts] are legally permissible, because to covet [anything] from them is to debase religion, since it leads one to sycophancy, compliance and collusion in their acts of oppression. All of this is a corruptive force to religion. The least harmful element of this is that when you accept their gifts and benefit from their worldly possessions, you begin to love them. Now to love someone is necessarily to wish them long life both in this world and the next, but wishing for the continued existence of the tyrant is to seek the oppression of those who worship Allah and the ruination of the world. What could be more harmful to one's piety and final judgement than this! Beware of letting yourself be deceived by the wiles of Satan or by those who say to you that it is preferable and more appropriate to start taking money from out of the hands of the poor and indigent; for [the rulers] squander it in sin and sedition whereas your distribution of it to the poor would be better. For the Cursed One [i.e., Satan] has cut many a throat with such malicious susurration. The damage he causes is pervasive, as we recounted in *Revival of the Religious Sciences*. Look [for the discussion] there.

(74) As for the four things that you should do, the first is that you make your conduct with Allah such that were your servant to deal with you in that manner, you would be pleased with him and not annoyed or angry with him, and anything that you do not find satisfactory about this theoretical servant of yours Allah as your true master would also not find satisfactory [about you].

(75) The second is that whatever you do to people should be what you would want done to you, because the faith of a believer is incomplete unless he wants for other people what he would want for himself.

(76) The third is that whenever you read and look into a field of learning, it should be something that improves your heart and cleanses your soul, as though you had learned that you had but one week to live – you certainly would not concern yourself with law, and legal disputation and theory, theology, and such things, because you would know that these sciences will not enrich you. Rather, you would pay attention to your heart, learn the characteristics of your soul, relinquish your ties to the world, purify your soul of its reprehensible traits, turn your attention to the love of Allah, to worshipping Him, and acquiring good traits. Not a day and night passes but that a man might not die in it.

(77) O Son! Hear another narrative from me and think about it until you arrive at a conclusion. If you were told that the Sultan was coming to visit you in a week, know that in the intervening time you would focus your attention on nothing but improving anything that you knew the Sultan's gaze would fall upon, such as your clothes, your body, the house and furniture, and so on. Now, reflect on the allusion, for you are intelligent and a single word suffices the wise. The Prophet (peace and

blessing upon him!) said: "Allah looks at neither your manners nor your actions; He examines your hearts and intentions." If you want to know the states of the heart, look in the *Revival* and my other books. Such learning is an individual duty while others are collective. Excepting the measure of what the duties to Allah produce, may Allah grant you success in obtaining it!

(78) The fourth thing is that you do not accrue of worldly things more than is sufficient for a year, just as the Prophet (peace and blessing upon him!) would lay in provisions for one of the chambers [of his house] and say:

> "Oh, Allah, make the provisions of Muḥammad's family just enough!"

He would not store up provisions in all of the chambers, but only for [whichever of his wives] he knew to be weak in faith. For any [whose faith] was certain, he would provide no more provisions than she needed for a day and a half.

(79) O Son! I have responded to your requests in this quire, so you should put them into practice. Do not forget me in your pious supplication. As for the supplication you requested from me,[53] look for it among the pious supplications [below]. Read this supplication in your times of prayer, especially in the remaining moments.

(80) O Allah! I ask of you perfect grace, abiding protection, encompassing mercy, and good health, the most bountiful means of subsistence, the happiest of lives, the most righteous behaviour, the most comprehensive favours, the most pleasant bounty, and the most effective benevolence.

(81) O Allah! Be with us and not against us!

---

[53] See above, paragraph 3.

(82) O Allah! Seal the hour of departure with happiness; fulfil our hopes in abundance; bind together our coming and going with forgiveness; make Your mercy our destination and return; pour out the bucket of Your absolution into the containers of our sins; bless us by rectifying our failings; make piety our provision – in Your religion lies effort and upon You lies our dependence and support. Set us firmly on the path of righteousness and protect us in this world from any cause for regret on the Day of Resurrection; lighten the load of our accountability, bless us with the life of the righteous, and save and steer us from the iniquity of the evil. Hold back our necks and the necks of our ancestors from the hellfire through Your mercy, O Mighty, Forgiving, Generous, Concealing, Benevolent, Omnipotent Allah!

(83) O Allah! O Allah! By Your mercy! O Most Merciful! First of firsts and lasts! O Most Powerful! O You who bestow mercy on the weak! O Most Merciful! There is no god but You! Praise unto You, that I not be a wrongdoer! Praise unto Allah, the Lord of the Worlds!

Tarbiya[1]
Dr. Amjad Hussain

Abstract:

This paper on Islamic Education is divided into three parts: an overview of the history of education in the Muslim world; an introduction to the different Islamic educational terms such as *tarbiya, ta'deeb* and *ta'leem* and investigation of the relationship between them; finally focussing on the importance of the *tarbiya* brought by the Prophet Muhammad ﷺ. It will demonstrate the importance of *tarbiya* in Madinan society which will be discussed in the context of the original pattern of understanding, upbringing and the cultivation of good character, highlighting how this edification gave the community of Madina the understanding, upbringing and character that today all Muslims aspire towards.

Aims

- To evaluate briefly the evolution of the sciences and educational institutions of the Muslim world throughout history;
- To introduce the three different terms used for education in Islam;

---

[1] Dr. Amjad Hussain, a lecture from the module on "Early Madina" at MFAS – The Muslim Faculty of Advanced Studies, Norwich 21/9/2013

- To understand the importance of *tarbiya* in the first community of Madina;
- To understand the social aspects of that *tarbiya* for Muslims today.

Perhaps the best way to define the general term 'education' is to demonstrate the relationship between the three indispensable foundations that make up the basic education of any civilisation, i.e. the teacher, the student and the aim or philosophy of the education provided. The term 'Islamic education' is sometimes misinterpreted when looked at from a Western point of view, for it is often misunderstood to be a complete interconnected system run by a religious establishment. In addition, the misunderstanding of the term 'Islamic education' is further exacerbated by the false impression that this kind of education only provides for instruction in 'religious' sciences and does not cater for the sciences that are not revealed. Arguably, this is not the case with education in Islamic civilisation.

In all examples of education during the early Islamic period, as in other civilisations, there was self-evidently a relationship between the student, the teacher and the philosophy of education. However, learning ethics, morals and the acquisition of knowledge (whether religious or not) were private and unsystematic activities. Hence, no single educational authority granted qualifications, even if they existed. Moreover, education was not under state control. It is astonishing that, in comparison with our contemporary period, classical Islamic Caliphal government allowed unprecedented and consequently unequalled freedom to the populace, as illustrated by the following text describing Muslim society during the classical era.

"Other than collecting taxes, the government did not interfere in the daily affairs of society. People were born, educated, married; they made their living and bequeathed their wealth; they engaged in trade and other kinds of business – all without interference from the central government. Virtually all of daily life was under the purview of Islamic law, articulated and administered by legal scholars who operated for the most part independent of the central government."[2]

According to most sources, the Muslims remained in Makka for thirteen years from the first revelation until the emigration to Madina. The political situation in Makka at this time did not allow the Messenger of Allah ﷺ to establish institutions of learning nor to have study circles openly. However, classical sources point to the house of Arqam in Makka, near the foothills of Mount Safa, as the first seat of Islamic learning. Arqam ibn Abi Arqam ؓ was one of the Prophet's Companions in Makka and his house was used by the Messenger of Allah ﷺ to teach Muslims about their *deen*.[3] Most historical evidence points towards Dar al-Arqam being used for three years before the infamous boycott of Banu Hashim, when it was finally abandoned. However, it is in Madina that the first Muslim *dawla* was created and therefore it was here that the parameters of the social structures of Islam were revealed. The first six months of the Prophet's residence in Madina were occupied with the construction of the Prophet's mosque and houses for

---

[2] Tamara Sonn, *Islam, A Brief History*, 2nd edition, (Oxford: Wiley-Blackwell), 2010, p. 50.
[3] Syed M. Naquib al-Attas, *The Concept of Education in Islam: A Framework for an Islamic Philosophy of Education*, (Jeddah: Hodder and Stoughton), 1979, p. 99.

the emigrants. On one side of this mosque there was a place that became used for learning, known as the Suffa. Hamidullah argues that the Suffa was not only used as a place for poorer Muslims to sleep at night or simply for those who wanted to lead a saintly life, but maintains that in addition to these uses it was also the first place of learning in Madina. Within a short space of time, education began in the other nine mosques of Madina as well, which had study circles that served in providing education for the inhabitants.[4]

From the city of Madina developed all the other education institutions of the Islamic civilisation. Throughout the different periods of Islamic history elementary schools entitled *kuttab* and *maktab* arose. However, these were all separate from each other and were mostly independent of state authorities. The historian Makdisi points out that the *maktab* and *kuttab* imparted such excellent training during the Islamic period that numerous students went into further study of the *adab* sciences, law studies and into government administration apprenticeship.[5]

At higher levels of education, especially in the early days of Islam, most students had to travel long distances to various scholars in order to learn from them. During this era of the early Islamic civilisation, the distinction between elementary education and higher education was very clear and the mosque was the main educational centre for higher education. The mosques were used as higher education schools to teach adults Islam and literacy. By the Umayyad period two types of mosques emerged: *amasjid*, the local mosque for the five daily

---

[4] Hamidullah, *Khutabat-e-Bahaawalpoor* (Essays of Bahaawalpoor), (Islamabad: Idarah Tahqiqat Islami), 1997, pp. 202-205
[5] George Makdisi, *The Rise of Humanism in Classical Islam and the Christian West*, (Edinburgh: Edinburgh University Press), 1990, pp. 40-50.

prayers, and *al-jami'* – the major mosque at which the *Jumu'a* prayer was held. The mosque curriculum grew to teach all the revealed sciences and the *adab* sciences. In the Abbasid period, the majority of the mosques of both types began to be utilised for study circles.[6] It is interesting to note that the English term 'university' is derived from the Latin, *'universitas magistrorum et scholarium'*, which can be translated as, 'community of teachers and scholars'. According to Hugh Goddard, the Western university is an Islamic innovation, in that the Islamic world was the first civilisation to introduce an institution of learning that centred on various faculties, as opposed to the learning of antiquity that centred on specific individual teachers.[7] Historically, the first specific higher education institution with a building devoted primarily to learning in the Islamic world was the *Jami' al-Qayrawiyyīn* in Fez founded in 899 CE by the Tunisian noble woman, Fatima al-Fihri.[8] The higher education institute of al-Azhar in Cairo was second in 969 CE, established by the Ismaili Shi'ite dynasty.[9] Al-Azhar did not become a fully-fledged *madrasa* of the *Sunna wa al-Jama'a* until the eleventh century when Sultan Salah ad-Deen Yusuf ibn Ayyub (1138-1193) conquered Egypt from the Fatimid Caliphate. However, it was during the early period of the Seljuk rule in Baghdad, that the first independent madrasa was instituted by the minister Nizam al-Mulk (d. 1092). By 1065 CE he had founded the Nizamiyya madrasa of Baghdad, and after this year, the

---

[6] E. Ihsanoglu and F. Gunergun (eds.), *Science in Islamic Civilization*, (Turkey: IRCICA), 2000, p. 1.

[7] Ibid.

[8] John Esposito, *The Oxford Dictionary of Islam*, (Oxford: Oxford University Press), 2003, p. 328.

[9] Hugh Goddard, *A History of Christian-Muslim Relations*, (Edinburgh: Edinburgh University press), 2000, p. 99.

pace of madrasa building accelerated throughout the whole Muslim world.[10] The higher education institute termed madrasa continued to evolve as an educational institution until the end of the Ottoman period.

Hence, it is important to recognise that the Islamic Education system has developed over fourteen centuries whereby educational institutions changed over time and evolved into other institutions with different curricula and administrations. In other words, Islamic education is the product of a fourteen hundred year old Islamic civilisation that spanned Arabia, Spain, India and Indonesia. The existence of this civilisation has meant that its teachings have been widely imparted. Islamic education has always been both unified in its worldview and at the same time diverse, due to variations in culture, geography and history. Islamic education is singular in its Qur'anic worldview, yet it still cannot be understood as a single concept but as a phenomenon with many aspects, all influenced by intellectual, social and political forces of its geography and time.

My recently published book entitled, *A Social History of Education in the Muslim World: From the Prophetic Era to Ottoman Times*, concentrated mainly on institutions such as the *masjid, al-jami', madrasa, kuttab, maktab, bimaristan*, the library and the chancery school (*diwan*), where knowledge of the various sciences, both transmitted and rational, was taught. This means that the book focuses primarily on the development of all the sciences found within the Muslim world, the imparting of this knowledge and the educational culture existing within Islamic civilisation. The book demonstrates that in less than four

---

[10] Ahmad Shalaby, *The History of Muslim Education*, (Karachi: Indus Publication), 1979, pp. 57-69.

centuries after the first Islamic conquest, jurists, scholars of the Qur'an and *hadith*, philosophers, mathematicians, botanists, physicians, geographers, alchemists and their peers in other scientific disciplines had accomplished the remarkable feat of unwrapping the vast intellectual legacy from past civilisations to create an Islamic universe which appeared orderly, functional and workable.[11]

Nevertheless, what needs to be acknowledged is that, while the concepts of imparting knowledge i.e. *ta'leem* and the learning of literature and social mannerism i.e. *ta'deeb*, have been dealt with in detail within the growing literature of education, the concept of *tarbiya* needs to be looked at in more depth since it has not received proper attention yet. It is very much true that the Prophet ﷺ was a model in respect of *ta'leem* and *ta'deeb* as he was in every other area of life. What marks out the first community is the fact that the city and its people were moulded, nurtured, given understanding and character by being in the presence of the Prophet Muhammad ﷺ. This is known as the *tarbiya* of the Prophet ﷺ. I would like to investigate at this juncture, the concept of *tarbiya* and how it impacted the first community rather than the emphasis on imparting knowledge, and the development of the various Islamic sciences, which was historically the second stage of Muslim Education.

Let us now have a closer look at the three main terms for education in the Arabic language. The majority of the scholars agree that three Arabic terms express the meaning of education in the Islamic sense. Two of these terms are taken from the Qur'an and the third is derived from the *hadith* literature.[12] The

---

[11] Howard R. Turner, *Science in Medieval Islam*, (Austin: University of Texas Press), 1997, p.33.
[12] Seyyed Hossein Nasr, *Traditional Islam in the Modern World*, (London:

first term *'tarbiya'*, which means 'fostering growth', derives from the Qur'an and its root is *'rabba'*, which means to 'cause to increase and grow'.[13] In the Qur'an Allah  says:

$$\text{وَاخْفِضْ لَهُمَا جَنَاحَ الذُّلِّ مِنَ الرَّحْمَةِ وَقُل رَّبِّ ارْحَمْهُمَا كَمَا رَبَّيَانِي صَغِيرًا}$$

"Take them under your wing, out of mercy, with due humility and say: 'Lord, show mercy to them as they did in looking after me when I was small'."[14]

Imam al-Baydawi (d.685 AH) described *tarbiya* as the nurturing of a person step by step until they are completed, akin to the way that the Lord of the universe nurtures His creation. The first term therefore indicates that Islamic education is there to nurture a person not only in in their youth but throughout their lives.

The second term for education used in the Qur'an is *'ta'leem'* and it comes from the root word *'ilm*, which means 'knowledge'. It has been used within the Qur'an as:

$$\text{الَّذِي عَلَّمَ بِالْقَلَمِ عَلَّمَ الْإِنسَانَ مَا لَمْ يَعْلَمْ}$$

"He who taught by the pen, taught man what he did not know."[15]

KPI), 1987, p. 123.

[13] Zaid bin Ngah, *The Practice of the Prophet Muhammad in Tarbiyah: Its significance for the formation of the first Muslim community*, (M.Phil: University of Birmingham), 1996, p. 34.

[14] Abdalhaqq and Aisha Bewley, *The Noble Qur'an: a New Rendering of Its Meaning in English*, (London: Ta-Ha Publishers), 2011, Sura al-Isra' 17:24.

[15] Sura al-'Alaq 96:4-5.

This term specifically means the imparting of knowledge. The last term, *'ta'deeb'*, derives from the *hadith* reporting that Prophet Muhammad ﷺ said:

$$\text{أَدَّبَنِي رَبِّي فَأَحْسَنَ تَأْدِبِي}$$

"My Lord educated me and then made my education most excellent."¹⁶

The root of *ta'deeb* is *adab*, which in a wider sense implies good manners and ethics. In addition to 'good manners and ethics', it means 'literature' or the 'literary and philological sciences'. In the Arabic language the term *adab was* originally used in reference to an invitation to a meal; it then developed on to mean an invitation to people to adopt the best of manners. During the period of the Umayyads and the Abbasids it became a term used for imparting knowledge of literature and displaying the correct mannerisms within the social sphere. In a wider sense this is how it implies good manners and ethics. During the 9th century the scholar al-Jahiz (d. 868) defined *adab* as an action which is carried out thoroughly with the knowledge of a wide range of sciences related to it. During the 14th century, the scholar Ibn Khaldun went on to define *adab* as knowledge of literature and skills in poetry and oratory.

We know that these three specific educational terms were not in common use amongst people at the time of the Prophet ﷺ;

---

¹⁶ 'Abd ar-Raḥmān al-Qāsim (**comp. and ed.**), *Ibn Taymiyya Fatāwā*, **Vol. 18, (Beirut: Dar al-Kutub al-Ilmiyyah), 1398 AH, p. 375 and also see Muhammad al-Zarkashi,** *Ibn Taymiyya Fatāwā*, **(Beirut: Dar al-Kutub al-Ilmiyyah), 1406 AH, p. 160.** Also see Syed M. Naquib al-Attas, *The Concept of Education in Islam: A Framework for an Islamic Philosophy of Education*, (Jeddah: Hodder and Stoughton), 1979, p. 144.

they were later coined from the Qur'an and *Sunna* by historians and educators who looked back to the sources and the earliest era of Islam for inspiration. This is also true for many terms that we use today for Islamic sciences such as the science of *tasawwuf* and *fiqh*; which existed during the time of the Prophet ﷺ but the terms to describe them were coined much later on in Islamic history. Therefore, *ta'leem*, *ta'deeb* and *tarbiya* were embodied in action and practice in Madina during the Prophet's time but were not articulated as a written educational theory. The traditions of the Prophet Muḥammad contain numerous sayings concerning knowledge, nurture and edification. He himself called upon individuals to educate themselves when he said, as is narrated by Anas ؓ: "The quest for knowledge is incumbent upon every Muslim"[17],[18] and on another occasion Abu-d-Darda' ؓ narrated that the Prophet ﷺ said, "The learned are the heirs of the Prophets, and the Prophets leave neither dinar nor dirham; they only leave knowledge, and he who takes it takes an abundant portion."[19]

Other *hadith*s specifically mention education in relation to ethics and manners, for example, 'Abdullah ibn 'Amr ؓ mentioned that the Messenger of Allah ﷺ neither spoke in an insulting manner nor did he ever deliberately utter evil. He narrated that the Prophet used to say, "The most beloved to me amongst you is the one who has the best character and

---

[17] Abu Muhammad ibn Yazid ibn Majah al-Rabi al-Qazwini, *Sunan Ibn Majah*, Kitāb al-'Ilm, No. 224, (Beirut: Dar al-Maarifah), 1996. Also see Muhammad ibn 'Abdullah Khatib at-Tabrizi, Abdul Hameed Siddiqui (tr.), *Mishkāt al-Maṣābīḥ*, **Kitāb al-'Ilm, Vol. 1, No. 218,** (Lahore: Islamic Publication Ltd.), 1979, p. 136.

[18] Both men and women are intended by the *hadith*.

[19] Abu Dawoud, Ahmad Hasan (tr.), *Sunan Abū Dāwūd*, Kitāb al-'Ilm, **Chapter 1369, No. 3634, Vol. III, (New Delhi: Al-Madinah Publications), 1985, p. 1034.**

manners."²⁰ The *hadith* narrated by Jabir ibn 'Abdullah 🌸 illustrates beautifully the meaning of manners and ethics in relation to education. Jabir narrated that the Prophet 🌸 said, "Enjoining all that is good is a *sadaqa*."²¹

Numerous examples of the importance given to the spiritual, mental and physical aspects of life can be found in the societal norms that Prophet Muhammad 🌸 imparted to the society of Madina. The importance of acquiring etiquette and manners is demonstrated in numerous books written by Muslim scholars throughout Islamic history, dealing with topics such as the correct courtesy due to Allah, the Messengers, oneself, parents, children, siblings, and the community; these scholars highlight the correct manners of cleanliness, eating, attending a gathering, travelling and even sleeping etc. The Prophet 🌸 taught his Companions to eat together when he said, as narrated by Wahshi ibn Harb 🌸, "If you gather together at your food and mention Allah's name, you will be blessed in it,"²² and he said to one youth when eating, as narrated by 'Umar ibn Abi Salamah 🌸, "Come near, my son, mention Allah's name, eat with your right hand and eat from what is near you."²³

[20] Muḥammad ibn Ismā'īl ibn al-Mughīra al-Bukhārī, Muhammad Muhsin Khan (tr.), *Ṣaḥīḥ al-Bukhārī* -The translation of the meaning of *Ṣaḥīḥ al-Bukhārī*, Book of the Companions of the Prophet, **No. 104, Vol. 5,** (New Delhi: Kitab Bhavan), 1984.

[21] Muḥammad ibn Ismā'īl ibn al-Mughīra al-Bukhārī, Muhammad Muhsin Khan (tr.), *Ṣaḥīḥ al-Bukhārī* – The translation of the meaning of *Ṣaḥīḥ al-Bukhārī*, **K**itāb al-*Adab*, **No. 50, Vol. 8,** (New Delhi: Kitab Bhavan), 1984.

[22] Abū Dāwūd, Ahmad Hasan (tr.), *Sunan Abū Dāwūd*, **K**itāb al-Aṭ'imah, **Chapter 1418, No. 3755, Vol. III, (New Delhi: Al-Madina Publications), 1985, p. 1063.**

[23] Abū Dāwūd, Ahmad Hasan (tr.), *Sunan Abū Dāwūd*, **K**itāb al-Aṭ'imah, **Chapter 1423, No. 3768, Vol. III, (New Delhi: Al-Madina Publications), 1985, p. 1063.**

The majority of these reports were recorded under the title *Kitab al-'Ilm* ['The Book of Knowledge'] or under the title *Kitab al-Adab* (The Book of Manners) in a variety of *hadith* collections, thus reflecting the intimate and important connection between character, good behaviour, courtesy and knowledge. The Prophet ﷺ did not focus on *ta'leem* and *ta'deeb* in a systematic and specific way, but rather it could be said that knowledge of these sciences was imparted in general under the wider term of *'deen'*. These uncategorised sciences at that time covered a wide variety of topics such as Qur'an, *hadith*, jurisprudence, worship, spirituality; indeed these were the basis for the entire Muslim civilisation. These were formally taught within the semi-circle, referred to as a *'halaqah'*. It was named thus because the teacher sat against a wall or a pillar and the students would make a semi-circle around him/her. The semi-circle was formed according to rank, thus the most advanced students sat closer to the teacher.[24] This unique educational experience was a constant phenomenon throughout the history of Islamic education, be it in the mosque, *kuttab*, *maktab*, or madrasa.[25]

Coming back to the term *tarbiya*, which is derived from the root word *'rabba'*, meaning to cause to grow or increase, it becomes clear that the general meaning of this term covers the other two specific educational terms, imparting knowledge i.e. *ta'leem* and refining manners i.e. *ta'deeb*. Furthermore, *tarbiya* also carries within it the meaning of an education that gradually brings something to completeness, perfection or maturity. This is exactly what occurred within the city of Madina during the

---

[24] Nakosteen, op. cit., p. 45.
[25] Munir-ud-din Ahmed, *Muslim Education and the Scholar's Social Status up to the 5th century Muslim Era*, (Zurich: Verlag Der Islam), 1968, p. 53.

Prophet's ﷺ life. Due to life and education in Makka being constrained by persecution, the primary stage of education or nurturing the whole community, began in what would aptly be called the city of the Prophet. The change of this rudimentary Arab society to a society governed by a written divine law, in less than twenty-three years, in itself shows the transformation the *tarbiya* the Prophet ﷺ brought, especially, during the initial ten years of the City of Madina. Hence, even though the success of *ta'leem* and *ta'deeb* is highly visible in the various eras of Islamic history, it is the *tarbiya* that the Prophet ﷺ imparted to the first community that must be acknowledged as the ground work of all education in Islam.

How can we begin to recognise this element of education, i.e. the role of the *tarbiya* of the Prophet ﷺ in relation to the first community? Perhaps the best example of the *tarbiya* of the Prophet is to be found amongst the customs of the people of the city of Madina during the first century of Islam. I find it appropriate to begin to describe the effects of *tarbiya* with an example from the life of the great Madinan scholar Imam Malik, who was born and lived his whole life in Madina. His legal theory strongly adheres to the idea that the customs of early Madina were the transmission of the dynamic societal norm, as set by the Prophet ﷺ; hence, the principle of the 'Practice of the People of Madina' was one of the main foundations of his legal method. Imam Malik grew up in a very knowledgeable household of Madina and the first example of *tarbiya* in Madina during the first century of Islam that I would like to use is that of Imam Malik's mother. Let us recognise the importance of the following wise words from his mother when Imam Malik wanted to acquire knowledge of his *deen* and asked her permission to allow him to go and learn. His mother accepted his wish but pointed out:

$$وقالت له: اِذْهَبْ إِلَى رَبِيعَة وَالْزِمْ مَجْلِسَهُ وَتَعَلَّمْ أَدَبَهُ قَبْلَ عِلْمِهِ$$

"Go to Rabi'a, sit in his company but learn first *adab* (manners and ethics) from him before learning knowledge from him."[26]

This highlights a very important aspect of *tarbiya* in early Madina which is that before learning the knowledge of the *deen* it is important to learn how to behave correctly with proper manners and etiquette within society. This is achieved through being in the company of good and knowledgeable people and learning the best of manners from them. It is important to note that the Prophet ﷺ was well known for his manners and etiquette, to the extent that even before revelation he was known as *as-Sadiq al-Ameen*, and after receiving revelation, when once asked how she would describe the Prophet ﷺ 'A'isha ؓ answered:

$$كَانَ خُلُقُهُ الْقُرْءَانَ$$

"His etiquette was the Qur'an."[27]

The only way that Imam Malik's mother could have had this understanding was because she was brought up and

---

[26] Muhammad al-Sheri, *The Concept of Tarbiyah by Imam Malik ibn Anas*, (Makka: Umm al-Qura, 2012), p.123.

[27] Narrated in *Ṣaḥīḥ Muslim*, *Musnad Aḥmad*, *Sunan Abū Dāwūd*.

nurtured amongst the people of Madina. This demonstrates that Imam Malik's mother represented the habits and customs of the Prophet's city as he had left it. *Tarbiya* means to have the correct manners (*dhu khuluq*) in every sphere of life but it cannot be simply understood as *adab* or *'ilm*. It seems from all the examples narrated about the Prophet's actions and teachings that *tarbiya* is the instilling in people, through informal teaching, such deep values as *hilm*, which means to be mild, lenient, clement, gentle, managing one's temper and to exhibit moderation. Other principles that were taught through his example to this first community were *rahma* – mercy, *haya* – modesty and shyness, *sabr* – patience, *tawadu'* – humility, *mazah* – happiness, *karam* – generosity and *shukr* meaning gratitude and thankfulness.[28] For example the Prophet ﷺ is reported to have said:

قال رَسُولُ اللَّهِ ﷺ مَنْ لَا يَشْكُرُ النَّاسَ لَايَشْكُرُ اللَّهَ

"Someone who does not give thanks to people does not give thanks to Allah."[29]

This *tarbiya* was taught to the people of Madina by the Prophet ﷺ throughout his time there. This means that while *ta'deeb* and *ta'leem* have a restricted meaning, the term *tarbiya* is comprehensive including within it both *ta'deeb* and *ta'leem*. However, it is important to understand that *tarbiya* is also very much the dynamic methodology of both how to learn and how to live your life. For example in the Qur'an even the manner in

---

[28] Muhammad al-Kandahlawi, *Ḥāyat aṣ-Ṣaḥāba* Vol. 3, (Beirut: Al-Risalah, 1999)

[29] At-Tirmidhī *hadith* nr. 1954

which to walk humbly on the earth is mentioned, which should be recognised as a form of *tarbiya*, Allah ﷻ says:

$$\text{وَعِبَادُ الرَّحْمَٰنِ الَّذِينَ يَمْشُونَ عَلَى الْأَرْضِ هَوْنًا وَإِذَا خَاطَبَهُمُ الْجَاهِلُونَ قَالُوا سَلَامًا ۝}$$

"And the servants of the Most Merciful are those who walk upon the earth easily, and when the ignorant address them [harshly], they say [words of] peace" (Al-Furqan:63).

Allah ﷻ also teaches humanity through the wise words of Luqman to his son:

$$\text{وَلَا تُصَعِّرْ خَدَّكَ لِلنَّاسِ وَلَا تَمْشِ فِي الْأَرْضِ مَرَحًا ۖ إِنَّ اللَّهَ لَا يُحِبُّ كُلَّ مُخْتَالٍ فَخُورٍ ۝ وَاقْصِدْ فِي مَشْيِكَ وَاغْضُضْ مِن صَوْتِكَ ۚ إِنَّ أَنكَرَ الْأَصْوَاتِ لَصَوْتُ الْحَمِيرِ ۝}$$

"And do not turn your cheek [in contempt] towards people and do not walk through the earth exultantly. Indeed, Allah does not love anyone who is self-deluded and boastful. And be moderate in your pace and lower your voice; indeed, the most disagreeable of sounds is the voice of donkeys." (Luqman: 18-19)

The Prophet ﷺ also said:

$$\text{إِنَّمَا بُعِثْتُ لِأُتَمِّمَ مَكَارِمَ الْأَخْلَاقِ}$$

"I have only been sent so that I may fulfill and complete the best of manners."

Conclusion

As said by Abdassamad Clarke:

"What was created in those ten years was not the 'Sunna' or the 'Shari'a' but a body of people who were dynamically increased in good character and trained to go forward and meet new peoples, new situations and new challenges. This was the supreme example in all history of *tarbiya*. The Prophet ﷺ acted as *murabbi*, fostering the good character and growth of his new community, as individuals, families, clans, tribes and as a society, people who when the time came were able to step forward and take the whole situation forward."[30]

The role of Muhammad ﷺ throughout his Prophethood demonstrates that *tarbiya* cannot be reduced to a mechanical process of training or indoctrinating, which would be a one-way transmission. On the contrary, it is a dynamic dialogic process which produces a qualitative change, such as that which can be seen in the early community of Madina. The Prophet's role amongst his people was that of a gardener who nurtured and cultivated his society in Madina; he nurtured a young sapling into a strong tree. *Tarbiya* as an Arabic word is often used in the context of nourishing the earth and the soil in order to grow and rear plants and trees. What we have inherited from the Prophet ﷺ is a dynamic process whereby we need to recognise that *tarbiya* is the embodiment of theory and practice. In other words, it is the informal learning of the *Sunna* of the Prophet ﷺ whereby it is recognised as not merely

---

[30] Abdassamad Clarke, "Madina: The New Matrix", Early Madina, the Muslim Faculty of Advanced Studies.

putting emphasis on the theoretical aspect of learning but rather the importance of the spirit of the *Sunna*. *Tarbiya* is the informal teaching, learning and practising of the *Sunna* which has been passed down through the various ages of Muslim history. It is not something that is merely taught in an institution nor is it something that is confined to a classroom or limited to the space between the covers of a book. It must be recognised as an organic living entity that originated within the city of Madina and has been passed down throughout the ages.

Tarbiya can therefore not be restricted to an age group or an élite group. From the understanding of the *tarbiya* of the first community of Madina, we must recognise that we all need to be reminded, nurtured and cultivated irrespective of age and the society we live in. From the example of the city of Madina we can learn that it is incumbent on us to develop our characters as individuals and as communities. However, learning that makes us static and not dynamic cannot be known as *tarbiya* since it leads to loss of reflection and understanding. As has been stated again and again within the Qur'an, *do you not think? do you not reflect? do you not ponder?* All of these reminders point towards the approach that the Prophet ﷺ cultivated within the first community, who never felt that their education was complete simply because they had reached a certain age or level, nor did they only understand education as simply literacy, knowledge, or manners but they understood *tarbiya* to be a constant quest of improvement for as long as there is life.

If *ta'leem* and *ta'deeb* are for the mind and the body then *tarbiya* is for the spirit; All are essential for the acquisition of our ultimate goal as human beings i.e. to know and draw closer to our Creator.

References

Hussain, Amjad, *A Social History of Education in the Muslim World: From the Prophetic Era to Ottoman Times*, London: Ta Ha Publishers, 2013

Turner, Howard R. *Science in Medieval Islam*, Austin: University of Texas Press, 1997.

Zarnuji, Burhan al-Din, *Instruction of the Student: The Method of Learning*, Chicago: The Star Latch Press, 2001.

Bildung and the Return of Culture[1]
Ahmad Gross

Plato's Socrates says: "Astonishment is the beginning of philosophy." For about 70 days now I have been walking up to this mosque of Granada in the morning and, having reached the Mirador San Nicolas, when I look out, I am absolutely stunned and amazed. Every single morning.

If those who have followed the previous presentations of the 'Jornadas Educativas' since 2009 or have studied them afterwards on the Internet were then asked to say something new on this occasion about "education" they would perhaps feel like me. I asked myself: What can I add to the great number of excellent presentations that have been acquired and formed by years of experience, work and existential learning? What apart from actions? An important, hopefully soon to be realised 'action' would certainly be to have a piece of land under our feet at last, and the means to tackle the consequent next steps, inshaAllah. But nothing happens without Allah's command, nothing happens before its time. One could also say that nothing happens without necessity. In German, the word 'necessity' *Notwendigkeit* is self-explanatory: It consists of the two words *Not* – 'need' and *wenden* – 'turning'. Only the need 'turns'

[1] 4th Seminar on Education, Granada, January 7th 2012

or alters the situation of a person. Heidegger said that "the true need is the lack of need." As long as people do not know that they are in need, as long as they believe their bad state of affairs is as it has to be, as long as they believe that there is no alternative, they are unable to alter their condition. Shaykh ad-Darqawi says in his letters regarding the highest need – which is for him the only true need: "Our master, may Allah be pleased with him, said, 'Had people known what secrets and blessing are to be found in need, they would not have needed anything except need.' He used to say need had the same status as the Greatest Name." When today's financial crisis, which in reality is a global system crisis, is seen in this light, it is in fact a blessing in disguise! By lifting the veil of the failed projects of humanism, atheism, 'enlightenment' and modernity, it forces us towards change, therefore, towards life itself.

About five weeks ago, in the 'Jornadas sobre Economia' here, we heard the shocking report of a Mexican member of our community about the so-called "peso crisis" of the year 1994/95 in Mexico. We heard about the dramatic consequences of the inflation for the people in Mexico: overnight, from one day to another, their money was worth nothing, hundreds (or thousands?) of Mexicans killed themselves, jumping from bridges and houses! Whoever has seen such a crisis in his own life – and not just on a TV or computer screen! – understands the real money of gold and silver, and values being part of a guided Muslim community, values the protection of our *deen*, and – at last – the true role of education as a means to freedom. Maybe some of us have asked ourselves: are we not turning in circles? What can one say about education that has not already been said? But, as Goethe said in his *Wilhelm Meister's Journeyman Years*: "All wisdom has already been thought of

– one just has to try to think it over again."[2] Moreover, we Muslims are very familiar with circular movements. At least once in our life, we gather together from around the world in Makka to make a circular motion around the House of Allah. In addition, this circular motion is also accompanied by the geometric coordinates of the line (the walking between Safa and Marwa) and the point (the standing on a point on the plain of Arafat). As long as we also set ourselves 'linear targets' and thus eventually also 'get to the point', we shall have no problem turning in a circle. On the contrary. The crucial thing is that we turn around the right things. Each thing has its time and coming to maturity. It is precisely this maturity which is our concern during these Seminars on Education. This concentration through encircling around our vision of an integrated school has now been continued for the past thirty years, both in theory and practice. In a letter Goethe has named this turning around the same theme 'to cohibit', using a term from chemistry[3]: i.e. to advance through an ever-higher concentration to the substance, to the essence of a thing. It is reminiscent of homoeopathy: to some people it appears as quackery or a placebo, but it helps others, by Allah's command. Sidi Ali al-Jamal[4] said words to the effect that the invisible dominates the visible. The ideas of the invisible *ruh* (meaning spirit in Arabic) call for manifestation in the visible world, for

---

[2] Goethe, *Observations in the Mindset of the Wanderers: Art, Ethics, Nature* 1

[3] "Confusing doctrine about confused dealing rules the world, and I have nothing more urgent to do than to intensify where possible what is inherent in me and what has remained with me, and to cohibit my peculiarities, just as you, my worthy friend, even in your castle are accomplishing." (Goethe's letter to Wilhelm von Humboldt from 03/17/1832)

[4] The teacher of Moulay al-'Arabi ad-Darqawi and author of *The Meaning of Man*.

the earth, people and their deeds. A Muslim should either be a student or a teacher, no matter where he is or happens to be. Over the years it has become increasingly clear to us that our school cannot be an artificial school-island but rather must be an "Educational City" in its best possible, literal sense: the Muslim city as a school of life. "Not just an educational group but a social nexus is required to fashion humans of quality."[5]

We all, as we are here, are that group, with all our merits and all our shortcomings. The title of my talk is 'Bildung and the Return of Culture'. You might have wondered how can one today seriously speak of "culture" if one looks at the state of our planet and the people?

Where does the term 'culture' come from? It derives from the Latin word *cultura*, which is a derivative of Latin *colere* ('live, care for, honour and respect, cultivate the field') and in the broadest sense it is anything that man himself brings forth creatively, in contrast to nature which is not created or changed by man. The Latin word *colere* comes from the Indo-European root word *kuel-* meaning 'to circle and to turn' (which again connects to the 'circular motion' and 'necessity' mentioned above), meaning 'busily engaged, industrious, occupied'.

The term 'culture', which came to mean the cultivation of the soul or mind, acquires most of its modern meanings in the writings of some eighteenth-century German thinkers (Kant, Pestalozzi, Herder, von Humboldt). Following Erasmus (16th century) and Francis Bacon (17th century), their intellectual concepts of rationalism set the stage for the coming atheism and nihilism of the 20th century and today. How? To use a proverb: their ideas and concepts threw out the baby (Iman in

---

[5] Ian Dallas, *The Interim is Mine*, p.20

Allah, trust in God) with the bathwater (corrupt and irrational doctrines of christianity): Allah, the Lord of the Worlds, the Creator and Sustainer of the Universe at any given instant, God was being reduced to a mere idea of pure reason, which – for them – needed to be proved to be believed.

Since they no longer had any religion, any *deen*, they made their culture their *deen*: philosophy and the arts. According to Rilke, all poetry and art wants to praise, extol. In the 18th century, Europeans forgot Whom they had to praise (i.e. Allah!). In the 19th and 20th Century, they forgot praise entirely. Shaykh Dr. Abdalqadir as-Sufi points out very clearly that when man believes he is the Highest, when creation assumes the attributes of the Creator, then the reality of the human becomes subhuman.

Today the greatest minds of Europe, thinkers, poets and scientists seem to confirm each in their own way a general intangible feeling: that 'the ship' is sinking. Who can say today that he is doing any more than 'to count the losses', as the well-known German playwright, novelist and essayist Botho Strauss (born in 1944) has put it? Or to meditate on 'the crack' in our liver, i.e. our mortality, as the other brilliant contemporary German spirit Roger Willemsen (born in 1955) does? Ian Dallas's book *The Interim is Mine* (published in 2010) on the other hand penetrates to the source of each culture (which is worthy of the name). It describes what is a prerequisite for any just society and this description is a synonym for high-culture: namely the generosity of noble people – *Futuwwah*. Every community and culture is conditional upon it. He describes where it comes from and how it may be promoted and preserved. This book does not merely 'count the losses', it also leads the way to an ancient wealth in ourselves. In doing so it also creates culture

– among other things – without ever using this term as it is commonly used. The word 'culture' only appears in two places in the whole book. At both points (pp. 19, 21), it is not to do with what we commonly associate with 'culture' – literature, music or theatre, etc. – but rather with marriage and the sexual practices of a society and its impact on their health. When I asked the late Sidi Karim Viudes, the thinker and architect of the mosque in the Albaicín of Granada, for his understanding of 'culture' he just waved the question drily away and recalled the famous saying, according to which Islam (or if you wish Sufism) was 'initially a reality without a name but which in the course of time had then sunk to being a name without reality'. The same could be said of 'culture': in all probability the more one talks of 'culture', the less one has of it. When he noticed my perplexity, he added that this term actually only came into fashion in the 18th and 19th centuries. The ancient world only used it – apart from 'cultivation' in the agricultural sense – to describe the education of children in school. I also looked into "Germany's best book" – according to Nietzsche – Eckermann's *Conversations with Goethe* (held in the last years of his life, and published four years after Goethe's death). In it Goethe says to Eckermann: "We admire the tragedies of the ancient Greeks, but in truth we should admire more the time and the nation in which they were possible, rather than the individual author." Every cultural, individual performance of the Greeks "pertains not just to individuals, but ... belongs to the nation and the whole age, and was actuated within them." (April 24, 1827). The importance of this social context for the life and work of an individual person is confirmed for me by a reference of Shaykh Abdalqadir to evidence from the famous

History of Rome of Theodor Mommsen,⁶ for which Mommsen received the Nobel Prize in 1902. Among many other things Mommsen observed in it, is that the state of culture in different periods of Roman history can be discerned from the respective quality of the coins which were used as currency. Good coins were always accompanied by a peak in cultural achievement in any given period. Debased, clipped coins on the other hand always manifested in times of cultural decadence in Rome. People are, how they (trans)act. Whoever turns away from his Creator, whoever believes he can exist without any daily connection to Him, without any worship of Him – since man is created to worship – will necessarily create his replacement gods, his pseudo-*deen*. Whoever is without a *deen* will make his culture a '*deen*'. To use the metaphor of a house: whoever confuses the decoration of a house with its mathematical law of statics should beware of the collapse of his house. May Allah protect us against ever confusing *deen* and culture. We have learned that the *deen* is not a culture, but rather a filter for each culture, which purifies and ennobles any culture. We now realise, more than ever before, that what had once earned the name 'culture' in Europe between the Middle Ages and the 19th century is today covered by the 'dust of usury' (as was predicted in the *hadith*) and the all-pervasive nihilism of today's *kufr*.⁷ In an unjust society, a society that monopolises wealth, there can be no culture that deserves the name of high culture or civilisation. From this we conclude that our school must also

---

⁶ Ronald Syme (1903-1989), the greatest classic historian of the 20th Century, was born in the year of Mommsen's death. His work, *The Roman Revolution* (Oxford 1939) penetrates into the obdurate, oligarchic power centre.

⁷ *Kufr* – the ingratitude that entails covering over the truth and results in unbelief and rejection.

be a school of *muʿamalat* (of how to transact, how to trade with justice), that it must be a school of *amr* – command, in order not only to teach the law and practice of *ʿamal* – action, work, behaviour – but also to enforce it. In short, we do not really want to talk about 'culture'. We want to have it. We need to talk about the structure of our *deen*, the socio-practical blessings of our *muʿamalat* in order not to build a crooked 'house'"

Let us now leave the concept of 'culture' and turn to Bildung.

Bildung

The German and Slavic languages distinguish between Bildung 'formation' and 'education', while in English and in the romance languages the word 'education/educación' is enough: Lat. *ēducāre* "to raise, rear, nurture, feed, raise up from a raw, natural state". In German and Slavic *Erziehung* 'education' is something that nurtures or rears a person from outside and so describes in particular the process of receiving a (school) education. Bildung – formation, on the other hand stands for the broader education which one undertakes actively oneself, that which advances the self on the road of self-refinement, purification and ennobling. Bildung means 'a taking shape', 'a self-making', the formation of something. The term 'Bildung' is related to the Greek concept of 'paideia'. Uthman Morrison described it in a very intriguing way.[8] Historically the word 'Bildung' was first used in the German language during the Middle Ages by the so-called christian mystic Master Eckhart (1260-1328). Bildung for him meant the 'learning of Gelassenheit', a term that may be translated by 'serenity/self-

---

[8] "The Essentials of Classical Paideia – in the Development of a Transformative Educational Model", p.149

surrender'. Heidegger used the term 600 years later as a key term in his thinking. Meister Eckhart understood Bildung as 'something pertaining to God', more than that – and here Muslims begin to shiver – 'in order that man resemble God'. *Astaghfirullah* – I seek forgiveness of Allah. When Master Eckhart speaks of *Nachbildung* – man's imitation of 'the form or image of God' (the *imago Dei* doctrine), then this concept is unacceptable to every clear intellect, in particular for that of the Muslim. Here is a source of dangerous confusion against which only the clarity of our *'aqida*[9] can protect us. Simply put: Allah is the Creator Who is independent of everything and the Lord of the Worlds Whom no form or image can ever encompass. The Creator is the Creator, independent of everything, sovereign and eternal. Creation is, on the other hand, totally dependent on its Creator Allah. Creation vanishes, Allah does not. The model we Muslims want to imitate is the model of the best of creation, Allah's Prophet Muhammad ﷺ. Through him we hope to get nearness to Allah. Europe after the glory of al-Andalus had to wait centuries to be able to see again the first glimpses of the light of the Prophet Muhammad ﷺ. The great minds of Goethe and Schiller suspected what Bildung – the highest formation of the self – could be. Goethe wrote two key novels which formed the basis of the literary genre of the Bildungsroman ('novels of Bildung/self-formation'): *Wilhelm Meister's Apprenticeship* and *Wilhelm Meister's Journeyman Years*.

Wilhelm Meister's Apprenticeship is Goethe's second novel, published in 1795-96. Goethe's first, *The Sorrows of Young Werther*, made him famous all over Europe at the age of only

---

[9] *'Aqida* comprises what may safely be said about Allah, His Prophets and Messengers, the angels and the unseen realms, both from a rational perspective and from the revealed texts.

twenty-five. Napoleon always had a copy of it with him. While Goethe's first novel featured a hero driven to suicide by despair, the hero of his second (*Apprenticeship*) undergoes a journey of self-realisation. The story centres upon Wilhelm's attempt to escape what he views as the empty life of a bourgeois businessman. After a failed romance with the theatre, Wilhelm commits himself to the mysterious so-called 'Tower Society', composed of enlightened aristocrats, educators. The motto of the *Apprenticeship*: "... to form myself, just as I am, was indistinctly my desire and intent from my youth onwards," wrote Wilhelm in a letter. Wilhelm's goal is to leave disorder behind and find order, personally as well as socially. Some quotations from the *Apprenticeship*:

> "One should listen to at least one little song every day, read a good poem, look at an excellent picture and – if one can make it happen – speak a few reasonable words."
>
> "If we take people only as they are, then we make them worse, if we treat them as if they were what they should be, then we bring them to where they are to be brought."
>
> "An astute man finds the best education during travel."
>
> (*Apprenticeship*, Vol. 2)

Wilhelm Meister's Apprenticeship is a story of education and disillusionment, a novel of ideas ranging across literature, philosophy and politics, a masterpiece that resists all stereotyped thinking. The novel has had a significant impact on European literature. It also represents one of the important moments in the 18th century German reception of the dramas of William Shakespeare. Shakespeare's works attained tremendous popularity and influence in Germany by the end of the 18th century. *Wilhelm Meister's Journeyman Years*, the sequel to the

Apprenticeship appeared in its first edition in 1821, and in its final form in 1829, three years before Goethe's death. The novel was greeted by mixed reviews in the 1820s, and did not gain full critical attention until the mid-20th century. Consisting largely of short stories and novellas woven together with two lengthy sections of aphorisms, and several interspersed poems, the structure of this novel challenged the novel form as commonly practised at the time of its publication. Rather than having a linear storyline it looks more like a mosaic, a collection of precious stones of wisdom. A major theme running through the novel is that of 'renunciation, doing-without'. The most famous section of the novel is probably the episode in which the protagonist and his son Felix (the happy one!) visit the so-called 'Pedagogical Province'. This is an area of education and learning with unusual customs, with its own pedagogical philosophy and methods. Music – singing in particular – is central to their education. Foreign languages, instrumental music, poetry, a distinct notion of respect – combined with elements of humility and awe – are at the centre of their guiding worldview. Some thoughts from this book, which are quite familiar to Muslims:

Niyyat/Intention is the Key for Everything

"In the works of man as in those of nature, intentions are really worthy of particular attention." (Observations in the Mindset of the Wanderers, no. 22)

Power of Yearning/Intention

"The desire to do something is a premonition of the skills one has…"

History
"The best thing we can obtain from history is the enthusiasm it arouses." (56)

Freedom Needs Self-Discipline
"Everything that frees our spirit without giving us mastery over ourselves is harmful." (65)

We Need Useful Knowledge
"The false has the advantage that you can always gossip about it while the truth must be used immediately, otherwise it is not there." (148)

Majority/Democracy
"Nothing is more repulsive than the majority: because it consists of a few vigorous forerunners, of rogues who accommodate themselves, of the weak who assimilate themselves, and the crowd who roll along afterwards without knowing in the least what it wants." (165)

Reality of Teaching
"In the smithy the iron is softened by blowing on the fire and extracting the superfluous sustenance from the rod; when however it is purified it is beaten and constrained, and through the sustenance of an extraneous water it becomes strong again. This also happens to a man by way of his teacher."(16)

Learning by Love
"We only learn from those we love."

Guilds: Learning by Serving

"The best preparation ... is the participation of the most insignificant student in the master's business. Preparers of colours have emerged as excellent painters." (8)

Knowing and Seeing

"One sees only what one knows." (Schriften zur Kunst, Propyläen, Einleitung)

Seeing is Higher than Thinking

"Thinking is more interesting than knowing, but not as seeing/viewing/witnessing." (analogous quote)

For Goethe Bildung was not a theoretical concept, but rather a vision of the highest possibilities of man. Like that he saw the 'Urpflanze' (primal plant) and the constant change, the metamorphosis, as a law of nature, rather than just reasoning about it or rationally analysing it. Goethe experienced that seeing/witnessing with the inner eye of the heart is the highest faculty of man.

Muslims who love Muhammad ﷺ know that seeing him is possible. This is the secret every human being contains.

Seeing the Best of creation ﷺ and – even higher – seeing the Face of the Creator Himself, Allah ﷻ – this was the source which inspired the best people, also the best educators, in world history.

To remind mankind of these greatest possible gifts is the highest task man can aspire to. Education which does not allow a way to these gifts, betrays man of his highest possibility. I ask Allah that we may we never forget it!

Conclusion

There will probably always be people who love the arts and all things that we have traditionally understood as culture – literature, painting, music, theatre etc. What is the role of poets, artists in general? For the poetic thinker Heidegger, it is to think and thereby give thanks, in German: *denken ist danken*; for the thinking poet Rilke it is to praise and extol.

Perhaps there is first a need for artists who take on the untenable status quo of usury, each in their own way, before we can get back to the fair exchange of trade.

Writers, painters, singers, dancers, poets, arise!

Who can show us the Achilleus of our time in his holy/sacred anger against the usurers?

Where is the Schiller of today to call out to us to fight against the tyranny of monopolized "markets" and for our freedom?

Which film director shoots a film today like Truffaut's "Fahrenheit 451", in which the dangers of a careless use of technology are portrayed?

Who – at last – shows us the beauty of lived justice? Today!

A contemporary of Goethe, Johann Peter Hebel, (1760-1826) said: "We are plants, – whether we care to admit it or not – which must rise through the roots from the earth, to bloom in the ether and bear fruit."[10] Let us blossom then!

---

[10] Hebel: *Sämtliche Werke, Ideen zur Gebetstheorie*, 3

Education and the Art of Matchmaking[1]

Uthman Ibrahim-Morrison

Introduction

Rather than an academic exposition of pedagogical theory, what follows is a series of observations drawn from many years' activity as a teacher, a husband, a parent and as an active community member, taking responsibility with others, to fulfil the social purposes of the *Deen* as far as possible. This must, of course, include responsibility for the transmission of these priorities to our children and succeeding generations. This is where the question of education (and matchmaking) comes into its own.

In case you are all wondering about the connection between Muslim education and matchmaking [apart from being a clever trick to pull people in!], I hope this will become clear as we progress, insha'Allah.

It is impossible in the space available to go into great depth, so I will touch quite briefly on five essential areas:

1. General background
2. Parental responsibility
3. Community environment
4. The 'community' of educators and students
5. Curriculum

[1] Ramadan Residential, Norwich, Sunday 28th July 2013

1. The Background

The upbringing that occurs within our consumeristic and isolated families, except by the rarest of miracles, makes it impossible to produce the young, free and dynamic beings necessary for the recovery of the *Deen*. What does emerge is an emotionally and socially inhibited individual, incapable of maturity, responsibility or spontaneous action.

Shaykh Dr. Abdalqadir as-Sufi has made the following key statements with regard to this state of affairs:

> "The human being is in the nature of his education, and please remember no education takes place in the school, some habits are acquired there and some information is received."

The award winning teacher, author and educational activist, John Taylor Gatto has defined the purpose of modern compulsory schooling as follows:

> "The inculcation of habits, fears, appetites and attitudes useful to management."
>
> "Well schooled people are trained to reflexively obey a stranger's commands and to continually seek the judgment of strangers."
>
> "Well schooled people have a low threshold of boredom – they need constant novelty to feel alive, with only the flimsiest inner life they must stay in touch with official voices through television, radio, internet, cell phone, commercial music and other commercial entertainments."

Education must provide a reliable path to responsible adulthood, the components of which form an uncomplicated whole, but which for all its simplicity has become hard to make out against the complex and fragmented designs of modern living.

Fully rounded adults will display the following features:
1. Being either male or female and evidence of maturity;
2. Affirmation of the unseen and adherence to the worship of Allah;
3. Expects to die;
4. Seeks and hopes for provision from Allah;
5. Protects and educates children;
6. Assumes personal responsibility for order in society and the welfare of others;
7. Freely accepts accountability for own actions;
8. Capacity for personal subordination to legitimate authority;
9. Willingness to oppose the enemy;
10. A discriminating intellect consistent with behaviour.

2. Parental Responsibility

AL-GHAZĀLĪ (*Iḥyā'*):

"Adopting an effective approach for training children is extremely important and necessary. This is because a child is Allah's trust which He has placed in the hands of parents. The child's heart is like a nice, clean and simple mirror which, while it is free of fixed impressions and shapes, is capable of accepting the influence of all types of impressions and influences and it can be inclined towards anything you like. Therefore, if good habits are inculcated in the child and if he or she is instructed in knowledge, then the child after gaining such excellent nourishment achieves the real success of this life and the life of the hereafter – and the parents and teachers of the child become entitled to a share in Allah's reward for the good upbringing of the child."

By the same token the opposite is true; the burden of negligence falls on careless parents and teachers.

"Every child is born on the *fitra* but it is his parents who make him either a Christian, a Jew or a Fire worshipper."

There can be no doubt that education in its true sense is a question of 'upbringing', and that upbringing has its foundations within the family. It is the product of the family's success or failure in this respect, which in Western societies is handed over to public 'educators' at an increasingly and alarmingly early age.

I think it is generally true to say that the family begins with marriage, but in another sense, because of the crucial role of parents and relatives in the arrangement and organisation of their children's marriages, it might also be said that it begins with the parents – also because the physical and emotional atmosphere of the family environment in which children are raised can have a determining effect on their future marital expectations, choices, attitudes and behaviour. As we all know, there is plenty of evidence to suggest that negative family legacies tend to be repeated from generation to generation. There is a world of difference between a married life which is a genuine partnership based upon the highest shared aspirations of the couple, on the one hand; and on the other hand, a marriage in which the couple collude in the creation of a conventionally acceptable trap, where suppressed emotional tensions, frustrations, resentments and dissatisfactions are never far from the surface.

Let us look at the case of the mainstream western legacy through the observations of Shaykh Abdalqadir:

> "The child today is born within the nuclear family because, as we know from the history of the missionaries, this has been imposed all round the world. The first thing we must recognise is that the modern child grows up in a kind of prison situation, with two prison guards. In fact they have an élite prison, because very often it is two guards for one prisoner, and there is good luck if there are other prisoners to share the aggression. What this means is you have two attachments and two wars therefore. This primal drama cannot be escaped inside that pattern. I am not saying it is good, I am not saying it is bad, but there you already enter a whole series of games that are a matter of life and death to the emerging child. The most serious one is where the authority lies. If the male figure, the father, is absolute master and his word is law, the child is already in a very serious, critical situation. If the mother dominates the household, it is in another drama. If there is the evolved condition or possibility that between the man and the woman there is collaboration, the child has a chance. If there is an imperial father and obedient slave wife, there is no hope. There will be sanity without hope. But the couple produce the evolved creature."

The simple truth is that the function of Muslim communities is to realise the purposes of the Shari'a completely. Therefore, the form and function of the Muslim family must be consistent with the achievement of these aims. This means that under circumstances such as those we now face, where the dominant social norms and pressures are pulling us in the opposite direction towards the ways of kufr, which will lead to the destruction of our children, marriages must be arranged with the informed and conscious intention of fulfilling the demands of the highest criteria, and hence the formation of couples whose collaborative unions will nurture the kind of children whose natural sense of freedom and spontaneity will not have been emotionally or psychologically short-circuited and whose education will have enhanced and refined the innate nobility of their disposition. The community as a whole, if it is to survive to fulfil its own highest function, has no real choice other than to make this kind of education the norm.

Shaykh Abdalqadir sums it up as follows:

> "The [...] non-collusive woman will dwell in the growth of her feeling life. This is the non-projective being present in her seeing, touching and hearing centres. Not "nerve feelings" but the deep seeing and touching and hearing whose expression is aesthetic, is beauty (both inwardly and outwardly) and compassion. This is the power, light and force of woman without which the man cannot reach to his higher aspiration. It is this that is short-circuited in the bourgeois family. So that all that is left to the woman is 'nerve based' feelings. The reality of the woman touching the petal of the flower; in seeing the light on the water; in hearing the song of the bird, is itself transcendent luminous being. And without it man cannot understand life. He will invent an atom bomb and not have any qualms. He will drop it and not another man will say a word. But if he was with that woman, she would say, "If you make this bomb, what will happen to the child in my womb?"

DH Lawrence made the following powerful statement:

> "But no man ever had a wife unless he served a great predominant purpose. Otherwise, he has a lover, a mistress. No matter how much she may be married to him… unless his days have this purpose, and his soul is really committed to his purpose, she will not be a wife, she will be only a mistress and he will be her lover."[2]

With the emergence of the kind of man with the temerity to speak the truth, whose outward project is justice and whose inner being is illuminated by this determination, will appear the woman who desires him, and they together are what Shaykh Abdalqadir identifies as the 'collaborative couple'[3].

This then is the essential aspect of matchmaking which becomes a parental responsibility when it comes to the selection of potential spouses for our children. The ability to recognise this high standard of compatibility and the willingness to prioritise it over any other is essential, because in essence it is nothing less than what Allah describes in His Noble Book:

يَـٰٓأَيُّهَا ٱلنَّاسُ ٱتَّقُوا۟ رَبَّكُمُ ٱلَّذِى خَلَقَكُم مِّن نَّفْسٍ وَٰحِدَةٍ وَخَلَقَ مِنْهَا زَوْجَهَا وَبَثَّ مِنْهُمَا رِجَالًا كَثِيرًا وَنِسَآءً وَٱتَّقُوا۟ ٱللَّهَ ٱلَّذِى تَسَآءَلُونَ بِهِۦ وَٱلْأَرْحَامَ إِنَّ ٱللَّهَ كَانَ عَلَيْكُمْ رَقِيبًا ۝

O mankind! have taqwa of your Lord Who created you from a single self and created its mate from it and then disseminated

---

[2] DH Lawrence, *Fantasia of the Unconscious*
[3] see p.105

many men and women from the two of them. Have taqwa of Allah in Whose name you make demands on one another and also in respect of your families. Allah watches over you continually. (An-Nisa' – Women: 1)

$$\text{وَمِنْ ءَايَٰتِهِۦٓ أَنْ خَلَقَ لَكُم مِّنْ أَنفُسِكُمْ أَزْوَٰجًا لِّتَسْكُنُوٓا۟ إِلَيْهَا وَجَعَلَ بَيْنَكُم مَّوَدَّةً وَرَحْمَةً إِنَّ فِى ذَٰلِكَ لَءَايَٰتٍ لِّقَوْمٍ يَتَفَكَّرُونَ}$$

Among His Signs is that He created spouses for you of your own kind so that you might find tranquillity in them. And He has placed affection and compassion between you. There are certainly Signs in that for people who reflect. (Ar-Rum – Romans: 21)

$$\text{يَٰٓأَيُّهَا ٱلنَّاسُ إِنَّا خَلَقْنَٰكُم مِّن ذَكَرٍ وَأُنثَىٰ وَجَعَلْنَٰكُمْ شُعُوبًا وَقَبَآئِلَ لِتَعَارَفُوٓا۟ إِنَّ أَكْرَمَكُمْ عِندَ ٱللَّهِ أَتْقَىٰكُمْ إِنَّ ٱللَّهَ عَلِيمٌ خَبِيرٌ}$$

Mankind! We created you from a male and female, and made you into peoples and tribes so that you might come to know each other. The noblest among you in Allah's sight is the one with the most taqwa. Allah is All-Knowing, All-Aware. (Al-Hujurat – the Private Quarters: 13)

إِنَّ ٱلْمُسْلِمِينَ وَالْمُسْلِمَٰتِ وَالْمُؤْمِنِينَ وَالْمُؤْمِنَٰتِ وَالْقَٰنِتِينَ وَالْقَٰنِتَٰتِ وَالصَّٰدِقِينَ وَالصَّٰدِقَٰتِ وَالصَّٰبِرِينَ وَالصَّٰبِرَٰتِ وَالْخَٰشِعِينَ وَالْخَٰشِعَٰتِ وَالْمُتَصَدِّقِينَ وَالْمُتَصَدِّقَٰتِ وَالصَّٰٓئِمِينَ وَالصَّٰٓئِمَٰتِ وَالْحَٰفِظِينَ فُرُوجَهُمْ وَالْحَٰفِظَٰتِ وَالذَّٰكِرِينَ ٱللَّهَ كَثِيرًا وَالذَّٰكِرَٰتِ أَعَدَّ ٱللَّهُ لَهُم مَّغْفِرَةً وَأَجْرًا عَظِيمًا ۝

Men and women who are Muslims, men and women who are mu'minun, men and women who are obedient, men and women who are truthful, men and women who are steadfast, men and women who are humble, men and women who give sadaqah, men and women who fast, men and women who guard their private parts, men and women who remember Allah much: Allah has prepared forgiveness for them and an immense reward. (Sura al-Ahzab 35)

هُوَ ٱلَّذِى خَلَقَكُم مِّن نَّفْسٍ وَٰحِدَةٍ وَجَعَلَ مِنْهَا زَوْجَهَا لِيَسْكُنَ إِلَيْهَا

It is He who created you from a single self and made from him his spouse so that he might find repose in her. (Sūra al-A'raf 7:189)

The second duty of matchmaking that falls to parents concerns introducing our children to the best available teachers, mentors and inspiring role models, and introducing them into the best company of people of good character. It is not acceptable that children are simply dumped into the school system, privatised or otherwise, or just abandoned to the nearest school that claims to be 'Islamic' or handed over to *darul ulooms* which have failed to adapt to time and place: for the child who has not been completely destroyed by the family, these institutions will finish the job – and it is the parent, not the institution, who is primarily answerable, followed by those in authority over the community.

3. Community environment

This is how the matter has been described by my esteemed colleague, Muhammad Mukhtar Medinilla of Granada:

"What we have to try to strengthen are the bonds of community cohesion, the social cohesion that in the West appears impossible to reconstruct. Islam and Muslims are the new 'social adhesive'. Western society has lost the battle against the individualism and social breakdown which have resulted from the 'welfare' state, but Muslim society can offer an example of community resistance.

"However desirable as a goal, setting up a real 'educational community' lies beyond the capacity of the modern school. It is, therefore, down to us since it is well within our reach. Our system, based upon the early traditions of Islam, has to be based upon a congregation of education and culture; a community education, not an education for the masses.

"What is important to understand is that the regeneration of society has to begin with young children, and with full commitment on the part of those that have the capacity, both by word and by example, to transmit this education. In the words of Nietzsche, 'What is needed are educated educators, noble and superior spirits that can affirm themselves in every moment by means of word and by means of silence, beings of a mature and sweetened culture, not these coarse 'wise' persons that colleges and universities offer today. The educators are missing, the first condition of education is missing.'"

Opportunities for instruction which are not available locally must be sought in other communities and the opportunity this presents for travel is itself considered a priceless component in a youngster's education. Clearly, the aim of teaching must be to achieve the maximum coherence between the three strands consisting of education, scholastic instruction and vocational training. This balance must be maintained quite deliberately by ensuring that education itself remains paramount during the scholastic and vocational learning processes, and demands therefore that the environments in which they are carried out affirm, reward and incentivise the pursuit of good character. We must accept therefore, that the highest standards of instruction will only be delivered at the hands of 'distinguished' adults who are both well educated and technically proficient.

4. The teacher and student body

A good starting point for this section is the following quote from the writing of Shaykh Abdalqadir:

"Education lies in de-programming the expected response, in redefining the decided definition of the authoritative other, in opening up the awareness of possibilities in growth, and in recognising the high-drive child early on in order to begin the conscious preparation of an élite. 'The education of the best for the safety of the rest' and in order that 'history should happen'."

By teacher and student body, what is meant is the setting in which the organised (as well as the organic) dynamic of transmission, inspiration and guidance between teachers and students, is intended to flourish. Schools as we know them represent the very antithesis of what is required. Therefore, the scholastic setting, that is not a genuine community in itself, must be situated at the heart of a thriving civic environment, without separation from its main rhythms and realities.

Although it may not always be so clear cut in all cases, evidence of the 'high-drive child' may be seen in this letter written home from boarding school by the celebrated warrior-poet, dramatist and daredevil, Gabriele D'Annunzio, at twelve years of age:

"By now you will have read my five letters, written in different languages, and you will have blessed me.

"Be sure, Father, that this is the only true sweetness, the only true comfort that I expect from all my work. Praise pleases me because I know that you will rejoice in it. Glory pleases me because I know that you will exult in the knowledge that my name is famous. Life pleases me because I know that mine must serve as a consolation and a support to yours...

"Yesterday, our Director heard that I had written these letters and sent you my work; he called me and told me that I was a good son, that I would succeed, that I was courageous, that you were not spending your money in vain upon me, that I was always affectionate, always courageous...

"Oh! yesterday, I do not hesitate to tell you, was the loveliest day of my whole life...

"My eyes began to shine, I felt my heart swelling deep within me. I felt that I was panting for breath, I felt myself suffocating and opened my arms wide, as though to call out to you, and hot tears ran down my cheeks.

"They were tears of joy.

"Oh! for complete happiness one thing only was lacking – your kiss!

"How good for the soul are these moments after the tempest! How light I feel, how peaceful, how happy! I see my future bathed in glory; and I could wish, were it possible, that the motherland, my fellow-countrymen, humanity itself, might merge into a single person, so that I might take them all to my arms, saying: I love you!"

As for the teacher, we must not be afraid to look beyond their professional experience and academic qualifications for evidence of the vocational spirit and the touch of the catalyst whose personal qualities of character and ability to inspire have the potential to propel the student into making new discoveries not only about his subject matter, but about himself and existence. The great German philosopher Friedrich Nietzsche expressed his own youthful hopes and expectations in the following way:

"When in my younger days I used to indulge my wishes to my heart's content, I thought that fate would relieve me of the terrible effort and duty of educating myself: at exactly the right moment I would find a philosopher to be my educator, a true philosopher whom I could obey without further reflection because I could trust him more than myself."

Futuwwa

By its very nature futuwwa is a matter that embraces the entire reality of education, life at home and life in the world at large. Therefore, it must be the defining feature which runs through every aspect of interaction between those who inhabit the community of teachers and students; that teachers exploit every opportunity which lends itself to the direct transmission of futuwwa, the traditional Islamic practice of inculcating in young men the values of courtesy, service, modesty, patience, obedience to authority, selflessness, courage, physical prowess, sensitivity to beauty, loyalty, companionship, concern for the weak, and generosity.

The following example illustrates the universal admiration and high value attached to these personal qualities. Sir Wilfred Thesiger, acknowledged as the last of the great British intrepid explorers, recalls:

> "When I joined them [the desert Arabs] I asked for no concessions; I was determined to live as they lived, to face the hardships of the desert on equal terms with them. I knew I could not match them in physical endurance, but, with my family background, Eton, Oxford, the Sudan Political Service, I did perhaps think I would match them in civilised behaviour. When the test came, with near-starvation, thirst that clogged the throat, weariness and frustration, it was humiliating to fall short. All too often I would become withdrawn and irritable when they entertained chance-met strangers on our dwindling rations; highly resentful when we stood aside, pressing them to eat more, insisting that they were our guests, and that for us this was a 'blessed day'."

5. Curriculum

The following core studies formed the basis for the curriculum of the Norwich Academy for Muslims:

1. Qur'an
2. Arabic
3. Sirah & Historical Studies
4. Grammar
5. Literature & Poetry
6. Mathematics & Geometry
7. Physical Education & Sports
8. Music Theory & Practice
9. Foreign Languages
10. Natural Sciences

It is important to emphasise that this is not merely a list of 'subjects' to be compared and contrasted with what may or may not be provided by the national curriculum. It is quite beyond the scope of this paper to go into any great detail, but it must be understood that the crucial differences will lie in the intention driving the entire syllabus, the underlying rationale for each line of study, the choice of teaching methods and materials, the qualities of character expected of teachers, and the respect and authority accorded to them by pupils, parents and people generally.

By way of illustration I will finish by giving as an example the pivotal position of language study in any curriculum we construct for the education of Muslims. In the section of *ash-Shifa* which deals with the Prophet's perfect qualities of character ﷺ, Qadi 'Iyad relates the following:

> "The Prophet's pre-eminence ﷺ in eloquence and fluency of speech is well-known. He was fluent, skilful in

debate, very concise, clear in expression, lucid, used sound meanings and was free from affectation. He was given mastery of language and was distinguished by producing marvellous maxims. He learned the dialects of the Arabs, and would speak to each of their communities in their own dialect and converse with them in their own idiom. He answered their arguments using their own style of rhetoric so that, more than once, a large number of his Companions had to ask him to explain what he had said."

Command of the spoken and written word has been one of the more serious casualties of modern educational priorities. Language is the primary medium through which we interact with each other and convey our thoughts, feelings and ideas. We depend upon it in its spoken and written forms in countless ways, therefore it can hardly be surprising that eloquence has been throughout history a universally admired accomplishment, with the highest premium being placed upon preciseness, clarity, beauty of expression and persuasiveness. Hence, the study of English places great emphasis upon the cultivation of the students' ability to express themselves fluently and correctly both in speech and in writing.

The neglect of language training reveals another serious modern casualty which has implications for the study of all other 'subjects'. This may be summed up as the failure to recognise the prior importance of acquiring the necessary proficiency in the use of the 'tools' that make the effective study of other disciplines possible. In support of such an important principle I would like to end on a lengthy but revealing explanation from the renowned writer, scholar and linguist, Dorothy L. Sayers in her essay "The Lost Tools of Learning":

"The interesting thing for us is the composition of the Trivium, which preceded the Quadrivium and was the preliminary discipline for it. It consisted of three parts: Grammar, Dialectic, and Rhetoric, in that order.

"Now the first thing we notice is that two at any rate of these 'subjects' are not what we should call 'subjects' at all: they are only methods of dealing with subjects. Grammar, indeed, is a 'subject' in the sense that it does mean definitely learning a language – at that period it meant learning Latin. But language itself is simply the medium in which thought is expressed. The whole of the Trivium was, in fact, intended to teach the pupil the proper use of the tools of learning, before he began to apply them to 'subjects' at all. First, he learned a language; not just how to order a meal in a foreign language, but the structure of a language, and hence of language itself – what it was, how it was put together, and how it worked. Secondly, he learned how to use language; how to define his terms and make accurate statements; how to construct an argument and how to detect fallacies in argument. Dialectic, that is to say, embraced Logic and Disputation. Thirdly, he learned to express himself in language – how to say what he had to say elegantly and persuasively.

"I recognise three states of development. These, in a rough-and-ready fashion, I will call the Poll-Parrot, the Pert, and the Poetic – the latter coinciding, approximately, with the onset of puberty. The Poll-Parrot stage is the one in which learning by heart is easy and, on the whole, pleasurable; whereas reasoning is difficult and, on the whole, little relished. At this age, one readily memorises the shapes and appearances of things; one likes to recite the numberplates of cars; one rejoices in the chanting of rhymes and the rumble and thunder of unintelligible polysyllables; one enjoys the mere accumulation of things. The Pert age, which follows upon this (and, naturally, overlaps it to some extent), is characterised by contradicting, answering back, liking to 'catch people out' (especially one's elders); and by the propounding of conundrums. Its nuisance-value is extremely high. It usually sets in about the Fourth Form. The Poetic age is popularly known as the 'difficult' age. It is self centred; it yearns to express itself; it rather specialises in being misunderstood; it is restless and tries to achieve independence; and, with good luck and good guidance, it should show the beginnings of creativeness; a reaching out towards a synthesis of what it already knows, and a deliberate eagerness to know and do some one thing in preference to all others. Now it seems to me that the layout of the Trivium adapts itself with a singular appropriateness to these three ages: Grammar to the Poll-Parrot, Dialectic to the Pert, and Rhetoric to the Poetic age."

The clear affirmation of much of what is said here is still preserved in the traditional methods of teaching the Islamic sciences and is, in my view, one of the more salient examples of how well placed we are as Muslims to identify and recover the best of what has been lost and neglected in the march of 'progress'. We must have the belief and confidence in our inheritance as Muslims to take up this task for our own good and for the benefit of society at large.

Islamic Education versus Assimilation
Muhammad Mukhtar Medinilla[1]

I would like to start with the first *ayats* from Sūra ar-Raḥmān and their translation.

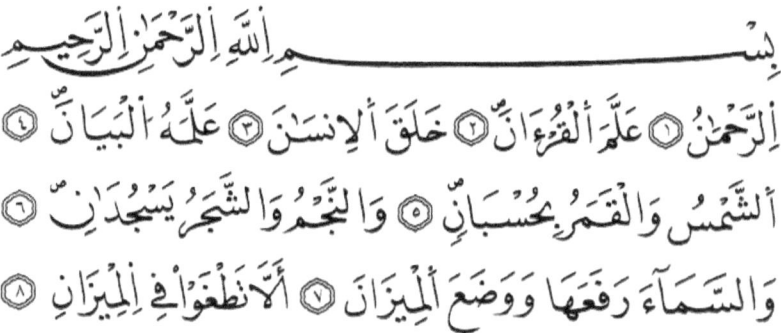

> *In the name of Allah, the Most Merciful, the giver of Mercy.*
> *The All-Merciful,*
> *Taught the Qur'an*
> *He created man*

---

[1] Translated from the original Spanish by Salsabil Morrison. Muhammad Mukhtar Medinilla gave the talk "Islamic Education versus Assimilation" in Granada on July 8, 2010, for the 7th anniversary of the Great Mosque of Granada. Abdassamad Clarke gave it on his behalf, as part of the module "The Question Concerning Education" organised by The Muslim Faculty of Advanced Studies, on May 2, 2015.

And taught him clear expression.
The sun and the moon both run with precision.
The shrubs and the trees all bow down in prostration.
He erected heaven and established the balance.
So that you would not transgress the balance.

Introduction

Insha'Allah, may all the lectures of these Educational Conferences serve in some way to make us stop for a minute and, in the words of Nietzsche (from whom I will quote frequently), "leave the frenetic rhythm of the epoch, which crushes and overloads us before we can even approach the major themes, pass... Sit down in the silent meadow to reflect on what is going on..."

In short, the main subject of this presentation is the unavoidable necessity of taking the matter of education into our own hands, the hands of the Muslims. This represents, firstly, a survival measure; secondly, the establishment of a means of perfection and elevation; and finally, the raising of a generation prepared for leadership.

Tackling education is a difficult matter because, on the one hand, the whole world has something to say about it, whilst on the other hand therefore, everything that can be said already sounds clichéd and commonplace. A return to principles becomes necessary, a return to the beginning, to recapture our meanings, as if we were starting afresh, as if we had just discovered them in all their splendour, full of sense and significance. My theory is that we need to elevate the degree of training, both in our own generation and in the generation of our children, in order to face properly the mission that awaits us.

When Miguel de Unamuno realised that his son, Fernando, would have to go to school, he wrote the following in a letter to a friend, "And to think that this human soul, because it is a real human soul, might be ruined in the hands of teachers and amateur educators – believe me, he will go neither to school nor college, no. I will teach him everything. I will have to learn it all over again."

"I will learn it again!" This is what I realised as a young man beginning to break away from the parameters in which I had grown up. I realised that I had to recover language again, recover the full meaning of words. Spain was in full political transition and I was feeling totally put off by the use and the abuse of these big concepts that had just become dull, tedious and unclear; in fact I was so tired that I used to carry the dictionary with me everywhere in an innocent attempt to recover the meanings of those big words whose meanings had been lost.

Perhaps we need something of this kind: to learn again, to recover afresh the profundity of key concepts and reactivate them in our present circumstances.

Now I bring to our attention the great German poet, dramatist, scientist and thinker Johann Wolfgang von Goethe. The three works that comprise Goethe's *Wilhelm Meister*[2] provide us with an autobiographical insight into an important phase of his own experience of learning. His protagonist, Wilhelm, often reminds me of our own situation. I see myself as a modern day Wilhelm Meister, yearning for instruction, for knowledge. Most of you probably also know Wilhelms who are equally thirsty for

---

[2] *Wilhelm Meisters Lehrjahre* – *Wilhelm Meister's Apprenticeship*, *Wilhelm Meisters Wanderjahre* – *Wilhelm Meister's Journeyman Years*, *Wilhelm Meisters theatralische Sendung* ("*Urmeister*") – *Wilhelm Meister's Theatrical Mission*.

learning, for knowledge and for elevation above the mediocrity that has dominated our upbringing within this system.

The day I finished my studies, the director of the teacher training college where I had been studying gathered us all in the auditorium and told us: "You have learned nothing here. I hope, if you are good, if you have good will, that from now on you will start to become teachers..."

The gift of Islam is enough for us and there is no better gift. Thanks be to Allah, Islam provide us with the motivation to take up the challenge to improve ourselves and to transform our lives.

Regardless of the amount of time that has passed, Wilhelm, 'William', remains a valid role model for us. A product of the bourgeoisie, he is subject to a succession of events in the midst of widespread vulgarity and mediocrity. From school he rises up from the lowest to the highest, experiencing the harmony of aristocratic life.

We now enter the body of the presentation, which is divided in three parts:

1. The circumstances;
2. What we should do;
3. Our proposals for and from Granada.

1. The circumstances

Well known western thinkers have clearly analysed what is happening. And in this regard, our teachers, most notably Shaykh Abdalqadir as-Sufi, especially in his works *Technique of the Coup de Banque* and *The Time of the Bedouin*, have provided us not only with the diagnosis, but also with the solution, the Islamic solution. I will only make, therefore, reference to the consequences provoked in the field of education and teaching by the current state of things, and later, to share some ideas on how we might avoid allowing education and teaching to suffer these consequences. In Nietzsche's *The Twilight of the Idols* we find this statement: "Goethe is not a German event, but a European event."

It has been said of Goethe that he was the beautiful singing of the swan, yet he was unaware of what was coming. Somehow, he did not belong to the world of the 18th century, nor did he belong to the new world, the one that had appeared as a result of revolutionary barbarism (let us not forget that he lived in the time of the Enlightenment and the French Revolution). William's perseverance in pursuit of perfection should have been comical in the eyes of the people of his time, as though he were being completely unrealistic, similarly perhaps to how people today might react to us.

What Goethe wanted was totality, wholesomeness. Nietzsche took the term "overman" precisely from Goethe. This 'will to power' of Nietzsche is so badly understood and negatively interpreted, especially by the humanists who only find in this concept the culmination of their own *shirk*, of their denial of the power of Allah. However, it is easily understood by the Muslim as the search for a more abundant, noble and sublime way of life.

If the overman is Nietzsche's ideal, the real human being seems to be the one who aspires to it, the one who occupies himself with the over-coming process, such as artists, philosophers and saints. He said, "At the centre, between the servants of the evident and the solitary, are the combatants, who are filled with hope."

To excel oneself, one owes to oneself 'to give form to their own character', including one's genetic heritage, parental influence and societal and educational conditioning. However, there is still a long road ahead. We are not a finished product; in fact, what we are now is barely even the raw material.

We need to work on ourselves, starting from the conditions we find ourselves in. Nietzsche cites Goethe as an example of someone who gave form to his character. Goethe was many things, playwright, novelist, thinker, scientist – but what Nietzsche admired him more for was this particular quality; he spent his whole life trying to make something of himself. I learned from Shaykh Abdalqadir that the first time Napoleon saw Goethe he exclaimed, "*Voila un homme*! – Look, there is a man!" From the many dubious unrestrained passions and wild ideas that he had in his youth, Goethe created a man, in the fullest and most authentic sense.

What Nietzsche could not explain was how those who came after Goethe, although they seemed to have striven to achieve the same as him, would not have obtained 'as an overall result – in his own words – "a Goethe, a healthy Goethe," but rather "a chaotic, nihilistic, lost and tired instinct..."

Nietzsche, as we well know, was completely against the idolatry of his time. Moreover, he was also able to see what the forces of the 'new world' were heading towards. In his book *On the Future of our Educational Institutions*, he reflects on the state of culture and education at that time, especially with regard to the secondary schools in Germany which were, at that time, considered a benchmark for the other nations of Europe. Nietzsche warns against losing the sovereignty of culture and putting all cultural efforts at the service of the state. The same is true of education; the aim of education should not solely be to serve the state. The Prussian state was one of the first examples of culture and education being used in this way and it can be seen again in another agricultural state, the USA.

Furthermore, it is important to understand that in industrialised England the function of the school as transmitter of family and societal values changes significantly from the late 18th century, with the French Revolution and the Industrial Revolution. Now, the need for centralisation and uniformity within both the population and the new economy determine the features that up to today define education. The state school system arises from the convergence between these political and economic interests.

A widespread misconception nowadays is the idea of the omnipotence reached by the state in the ancient Greek city-states. Our excuse for doing what we do is because that is how it used to be with the ancient Greeks. However, their state completely avoided this utilitarianism, which consists of accepting culture only insofar as it benefits the state and being rid of anything that does not serve its own purposes.

There is also confusion about the sense of the Greek 'Paideia' and its alleged analogy with democracy. This is happening today and it is especially within the world of journalism that this fraud is generated: Greek Paideia as a fundamental paradigm of democracy.

The journalist is the slave of the present, the slave of the moment. This is what has replaced the great Nietzschean genius, the genius that liberates one from the present. Journalism is the definition of and the visible locus where the two great evils against which Nietzsche warned us are united. In his time the matter was at its beginning, today we can see it in its completion; what he warned us against has now arrived.

These are, in fact, two dangerous tendencies of which Nietzsche was already warning us in his time. On the one hand, the extension and distribution of culture to everybody and, on the other, the restriction and weakening of the very same culture. The process of the last two hundred years leaves us, today, in a situation that is out of balance. In an article entitled "Culture and Depression", recently published in the Spanish press, a columnist raised a question which he himself acknowledged was maddening and absurd:

> "What if in the world of culture, just as is happening in the world of business, we were just playing with purely speculative values? What if we were raising artificially, in the 'Stock Exchange', the price of a few very damaged, dubious products? ... The blame for these ideas would have to be attributed to all the propagandists who have spent years trumpeting the 'economic value' of cultural goods, and who have insisted upon making culture a business arena comparable to any other, with the same parameters, the same measure: the millions it moves. What if we have misleadingly inflated the value of some cultural products while diminishing the importance of the limited number of works that truly represent a vital experience and contain a genuine wealth of knowledge about human existence?"

I have had the opportunity to read many reports, signed by professionals, reflecting upon this question: the suitability of education to the market and the commercialisation of higher education in Europe. For example, in his report "Neo-Liberal Globalisation and the LOE" (an acronym for the most recent Spanish educational law), Enrique Javier Díaz Gutiérrez, professor of Didactics at the University of León, concludes as follows: "In education, the discussion does not focus anymore on a liberating syllabus, based on achieving the vital development of our pupils that guarantees them full citizenship and real participation in the construction of a just society, but in a syllabus suited to the job market, in order to increase international competitiveness and profit." There are many similar quotations too numerous to include here.

However, our Education Minister, Ángel Gabilondo, has stated: "The social aspect of education is crucial in order to guarantee the European economic recovery process [as well as] to secure the social status of Europe and to legitimise the European model we want to construct.... A universal education, with quality and fairness, is the best option against unemployment."

As a result, one is quite repelled by everything that comes out of the mouths of politicians, at a regional, national and European level; they have even put together a "council of wise men," including Felipe González, former prime minister of Spain, to remind us of the importance of raising our standards of education and training in order to be able to become more competitive.

After declarations of good, charitable intentions, the universities and centres of higher education, such as ESADE or the University of Georgetown, controlled by Jesuits, prepare the new economic leaders. They study philosophy, but not to recover the Greek pursuit of virtue, or out of love of a classical education, but merely to improve their negotiating skills as a tool for use in the business sector. By the way, Javier Solana, ex-foreign affairs representative of the European Union, works at present for ESADE (private Spanish institution). The following headline appeared in the press just recently: "Javier Solana claims for Europe the role of 'world government laboratory.'" Of course, he is strongly in favour of 'evolving' the concept of sovereignty.

It is a curious fact that in the whole of Spain there is not one single university among the world's top hundred; but, nevertheless, it has three business schools in the top fifteen worldwide.

Today 'well-intentioned' academic multiculturalism declares pathetically, throughout the universities, the destruction of centralisation, of totalitarianism, and praises the cultural globalisation of 'their' culture (or should we say, their lack of culture) while the pretence remains that school gives shape to, and implements everything that in reality society cannot. The great ideals of tolerance, democracy and equality are simply ignored in the 'real' world, but they have to be imposed in the schools and 'transmitted' without the essential element that is the necessary example of society as a whole. Schools are legally obliged to uphold that which has clearly failed to occur in wider society, and as time goes on, the absolute contradiction between the declared ideal and the reality becomes ever clearer. The distribution of a common culture for all, which Nietzsche warned us against, along with the decline in the quality of education, has today resulted in what they define as the 'caring school'.

When you hear the phrase 'caring school', you are bound to say, "That sounds good, what an excellent idea!" However, it is not a model that encourages the development and use of the intellect, nor is it, in fact, one that seeks to promote care, or therefore, a capacity for empathy. In fact, the implication and undertone of the phrase 'caring school' has very little to do with caring in the sense of empathy, rather it is simply to care in the sense of 'inclusion' or 'containment'. Namely, the caring school is the one that can 'encompass' everyone. Everyone and anyone can be stuffed into it and its aim is simply to keep them all gathered together. This caring, inclusive school, in fact, ends up excluding 31% of its students, who are destined for academic failure. In Ceuta and Melilla, two Spanish territories with a strong Muslim presence, this academic failure 'targets' more than 50% of the school population, mostly the Muslim population, and therefore does NOT include, but rather abandons them.

This is the model that is being followed. The Spanish Minister of Education, Mr. Gabilondo, declares that it is not a question of standardising according to the lowest common denominator, but this is exactly what is happening.

In an extreme way, the evils announced by Nietzsche have taken shape, obviously not only in Europe:

- The inadequate teaching of language;
- Ignorance of the classical languages and lack of connection to the mother tongue;
- The 'free expression of personality' without an adequate under-standing of 'personal autonomy';
- Contempt for the importance of guidance as part of education;
- The erosion of clear cultural references;
- The break with classical antiquity;
- The corruption of art;
- The deterioration of philosophy and thought.

I was impressed by Heidegger's affirmation, quoted by Abu Bakr Rieger in the speech he gave in 2005 on the occasion of the opening of Dallas College, in which he announced "the end of the Age of Education in Europe." In the same talk, commenting on the insight of Jean-Christophe Rufin, medical doctor and political expert, into the capacity of democracy to assimilate and its need to gain political strength through confrontation with an enemy, despite its apparent weakness, he explained, "this absolute integrative power of the democracies has now led to the states becoming increasingly involved in the education and 'cultivation' of the Muslims. This state of affairs is of course provoked all the more by the recognition that only the Revelation escapes total integration."[3]

The general conclusion of most studies and reports about the presence of Muslims in Europe, originating from the widest possible spectrum of sources, is clear: in spite of the complexity and variety of communities and individuals, the adaptation and integration of the Muslims will never result. Alhamdulillah!

Assimilation is a concept that we instinctively reject. The meaning of the word is very clear: 'To make equal', to 'make alike', 'to make something external, something that comes from outside, similar to the existing reality.' We could even be more precise by using the Spanish term 'asimilismo': a policy that aims to suppress the peculiarities of minorities in order to favour the homogeneity of a society and thus establish the unity of the state on the basis of a single legislation, a single manner and a single identity.

2. What we should do

"The Age of the Republic has ended. The Age of the Princes has begun!" With this Shaykh Dr. Abdalqadir closes the introduction to his book *The Muslim Prince*. He declares it, "...a guide for the young leader of a new society as he emerges into sunlight and leaves behind the smoking, burning ruins of two hundred years of darkness."

It is essential that we reflect on our goals, as Shaykh

---

[3] https://shaykhabdalqadir.com/dallas-college-opening-address-by-rais-abu-bakr-rieger/

Muhammad al-Kasbi, imam of the Granada Mosque, reminded us in a class only one month ago. We must know what it is that we want and then we can focus on the means to achieve it. Those means, he said, can be varied (and I would add, undoubtedly, according to each community's circumstances).

He also said that our schools have to be informed by an awareness that we, as Muslims, have two very clear goals:

- To obtain the Garden
- To govern the Earth

Our schools and educational projects in general have to be 'schools of leadership', because, as Shaykh Muhammad said, you cannot separate the aim of gaining the Garden from the responsibility of the *khilafa* of Allah on Earth, our responsibility for governance. It is not so much a question of Islamic education being in opposition to assimilation, but rather, a question of Islamic education and the regeneration of Europe and the rest of the world.

What we have to try to strengthen are the bonds of community cohesion, the social cohesion that in the West appears impossible to reconstruct. Islam and Muslims are the new 'social adhesive'. Western society has lost the battle against the individualism and social breakdown which have resulted from the 'welfare' state, but Muslim society can offer an example of community resistance.

However desirable as a goal, setting up a real 'educational community' lies beyond the capabilities of the modern school. It is, therefore, down to us since it is well within our reach. Our system, based upon the early traditions of Islam, has to be based upon a conjoining of education and culture; a community education, not an education for the masses.

What is important to understand is that the regeneration

of society has to begin with young children, and with full commitment on the part of those that have the capacity, both by word and by example, to transmit this education. In the words of Nietzsche, "What is needed are educated educators, noble and superior spirits that can affirm themselves in every moment by means of word and by means of silence, beings of a mature and sweetened culture, not these coarse 'wise' persons that colleges and universities offer today. The educators are missing, the first condition of education is missing." These are educators who are aware that, as Oscar Wilde said, "Instruction is something admirable, but the most important things in life cannot be taught, they can only be found."

We need educated educators because we need guidance. There is a need for guides in the upbringing of our young people "...at that stage in life," as Nietzsche wrote in *The Future of our Educational Institutions*, "when the young person sees his experiences wrapped, as it were, in a metaphysical rainbow, in the sense of being out of their reach and difficult to understand; when man feels the supreme need for a hand that guides him." At this crucial moment in the life of a young person, modern society, including the education system, leaves its youth alone, stranded, abandoned to themselves to achieve their own 'autonomy', to be 'free', so that they can give 'free expression' to their personality.

The entire education system is a long 'linear' process, the sole aim of which is a place at university. Every day there are more degrees and every day more are needed; master's degrees, PhDs and more, all in order to be able to gain access to a job. We have to think of an educational alternative; the current situation of informal Islamic home education, as opposed to formal education at the hands of the state, is not the solution.

We should not use up our energies, so necessary for activity and creativity, in this exhausting effort.

At this point, we need to mention the fundamental role of the high school, particularly the baccalaureate, in what must be our future target of establishing a solid educational system in Europe, one that the kuffar will have no choice but to sanction. We mustn't underestimate the importance of the high school, the secondary cycle of education that is so crucial in the formation of future generations, since it will represent the real cultural foundation for the majority, as well as being a solid base for those who will eventually end up in university.

I am not speaking about scholastic education nor, much less, about creating an academic caste. I am speaking only of looking for the right form, of finding a way, in this time and place, to develop our own educational model; one that will allow us in the near future to establish the *ijaza*, the personal accreditation between pupil and teacher; not between student and institution. An *ijaza* is the certificate by which a teacher recognises and authorises his pupil to exercise or teach a certain discipline. We must establish a flexible organisation, adapted to the rhythms of learning and to the growth of every individual learner. We must recover traditional teaching methods, the circles of knowledge, a system of arbitration and interdisciplinary meetings, amongst other things.

However, this will be difficult if all this is not accompanied, in this non-cultural age, by the recovery of an authentic culture, "that culture that begins precisely from the moment in which one can treat what is alive like something alive." (Nietzsche)

If you are wondering then what the culture of Islam is, I have learnt from my teacher, Shaykh Dr. Abdalqadir as-Sufi, that Islam is a 'filter' for culture. We do not need to replace our own western culture, but we must rescue it, we must 'cleanse' it.

Education needs a context. Among other things, it also needs the recovery of classical culture: the Greek and European mythology that preceded the arrival of Christianity. There was a time, about twenty years ago, when Shaykh Abdalqadir found me reading a chapter of *The Hobbit* to the children and he said to me, "What are you doing? We have to recover pre-Christian mythology, because it retains certain values, values that are complementary to the *Deen*." We cannot recapture this model of education without, at the same time, recovering its cultural components: literature, narrative, art and philosophy; philosophy as education for the spirit.

To me, the difference is not between modern education and traditional education, but between good and bad education. The great Turkish *'alim* and sufi, Bediuzzaman Said Nursi, with the support and financing of Sultan Reshad, embarked upon the establishment of a university in the East of Anatolia, which effort was brought to an end by the advent of the First World War. Following his syllabus, we have to merge three educational systems into one:

- Modern education (*mektebe*)
- The traditional Islamic sciences (*madrasa*)
- Sufism (*zawiye*)

As for Sufism and the zawiyas run by the tariqas, I would like to point out that even today one is amazed by the fact that in the whole of the African Maghrib, especially in the south, the standard of literacy was higher and more widespread before colonisation than it has ever been since.

To establish a new educational method today also means confronting the question of creativity, because to develop talent is not a mechanical process, but an organic one. We return to the beginnings, to agriculture, hence the word culture: to tend with care. I believe that a concept exists in the very precise German expression *"Hegen und Pflegen"*, which comprises both caring for the person and recognising their talents.

"The current educational system mines our minds in the same way in which we extract minerals from the ground," says Kim Robinson, a contemporary educational expert from Liverpool, who was also a schoolmate of several members of the Beatles. He points out that Paul McCartney hated music class and nobody in his school seemed to recognise his musical talent. Kim Robinson is now an authority on the matter of creativity in education, one of his key observations being that our schools and educational projects have to be those in which our children are in their own element, like fish in water.

It is not a matter of placing alongside the word *school* the adjective *Islamic*, but rather, establishing a new liberating school, a transformative school, one that allows every youngster to be 'in their element', and that instils in our youth a yearning for knowledge, without losing a single speck of *tawhid*.

At the end of the 19th century Miguel de Unamuno wrote the novel *Love and Pedagogy*, in which he brought out the contrast between love, heredity and tradition on the one hand, and pedagogy, adaptation and progress on the other. That is, he highlighted the contradiction inherent in the approach of scientists and pedagogues operating in an empty modern world separated from real existence, obsessed with their methods, formulae and classifications as the means to reveal the secret of life whereas they are being taken further and further away from it.

We are not opposed to the science of pedagogy. In the hands of the Muslims, any pedagogical method, be it Pestalozzi, Steiner or Montessori; any of them can be put into practice with enormous benefit. In the hands of the Muslims all the pedagogical ideals find their just measure, their opportunity for application in the real world. As they say, every instrument sounds good when the score is good.

The way outlined by Shaykh Abdalqadir in his books *Tawhid*, *Hubb*, *Amal* and *Safar* indicates to us the order that our schools should follow:

First of all, the child has to find, both in school and in life, Unity-Tawhid. This leads to Love-Hubb (love is assumed at all times, because for the teacher love is like courage for the soldier, it is always assumed). This, in turn, leads to Action-Amal and this to Travel-Safar. I remember the educational programme Shaykh Abdalqadir outlined at the beginning of the Maestranza of Granada approximately twenty years ago, culminating with the departure of the boys out into the world on a journey.

Shaykh Muhammad al-Kasbi pointed out to us that Iman is half gratitude and half patience. This should inspire us to discover and to encourage the talents and qualities of the new generations and to have the patience to prepare them properly and instil in them confidence in Allah, and in their parents and teachers.

The relationship of teacher and pupil should be based on example. This is illustrated in the teaching transaction between Allah ﷻ and Adam ﷺ. Also, it finds its true meaning in the Revelation, and in the conduct of the Prophet Muhammad ﷺ, who said: "*Qul amantu billahi, thumma-staqim* – Say: I believe in Allah, then go straight."

It is the inseparable relationship between Iman and knowledge, between knowledge and usefulness, between *Adab ad-dunya* and *Adab ad-Din*. The core of this teaching, which is always education, this knowledge, which is always linked to an integral and balanced education – the true meaning of Greek paideia – is the mosque, because the function of the school does not consist of satisfying the requirements of a state ideology, but is directly related to *'ibada*, the worship of the Creator.

3. Our proposal

When I first learnt of the title for these Educational Conferences, 'Expectations of Islam in Europe', I quickly went, as in my youth, to the dictionary and looked up the definition of the word 'expectation' and found: hope of obtaining a thing, if the desired opportunity is provided.

Let us be seekers of opportunities. Let us be expectant, like those who wait watchfully, wide-awake, on the lookout for what they are certain is coming, who act with hope in an epoch defined by the absence of expectations, lack of motivation and conformism, which it seems, is the result of the proclaimed victory of the so-called 'western system' through its spectacular and progressive development of capitalist managerial methods. Shaykh Abdalqadir's observation about this scepticism is compelling: "Scepticism is nothing but fear."

In fact, instead of "Islamic Education versus Assimilation", the title of this lecture could have been "Hope versus Despair" or "Hope versus False Expectation". In other words, submission to the will of Allah and implementation of the *Deen* of Islam, following the guidance of the Messenger of Allah ﷺ, as opposed to assimilation into the *kafir* system.

"For Allah nothing is impossible. Allah does what He wills.

You can be a Muslim in any place and situation." These were words of Shaykh Muhammad al-Kasbi, who later added, "And let us try to correct and to improve (our own behaviour) as much as we are able."

Our expectations must be high and the projects that we embark upon must be great. However, the methodology, as our people of knowledge teach us, consists of advancing step by step in an orderly manner, while overcoming and elevating the circumstances. In the field of education it consists of establishing charitable foundations (*awqaf*), schools and other educational centres in accordance with the laws of each land, and in accordance with the particular features of each community. We will then grow in strength until we gradually develop a firm and well-established network across the whole of Europe; a network of collaboration, cooperation and convergence. This will be in close connection with the rest of the Umma, particularly with the Maghrib, Turkey and the Balkans.

Our proposal and our determination (the first to be in our community, among many other important proposals) is for 'The School of the Shaykh'. Shaykh Abdalqadir has transmitted to us his knowledge and his *idhn* for many years and our Amir, as soon as the mosque was completed, took up this task with great courage. Together we now have a team that is becoming larger and more determined every day.

Our proposal is that we work together, the Muslims of this city and those outside of it, and make the school our own. We are aware that no institution can transmit nobility by itself; that is something that can only happen in a clean society, as our Shaykh has made clear.

The one thing I wish to emphasise is that this project will require the help and participation of other communities, particularly with respect to secondary education and the future establishment of a boarding school. The prospect of a boarding school is a challenging but pivotal element, and is essential if we are to reach the highest possible standards of excellence.

Conclusion

I remind myself of the words of Sidi Karim Viudes, architect of the new Granada Mosque, during the Educational Seminar held in Granada in January 2010: "The future of Islam remains to be created; the opening is enormous. The future is completely open. The Islam that has to come to Europe will surprise us, it does not necessarily have to be just like what we have had until now."

That is why, in the end, I would like to evoke the figure of Goethe once again as a stimulating reminder for us of the Wilhelms of this age. In his search he managed to attain a correct view of the sciences and nature. He immersed himself in life, in his own circumstances; he looked for wholeness and shaped himself completely, uniting all the aspects of his being.

Inspired by the real suicide of a young man because of passionate love, Goethe wrote a novel that we all know, *The Passion of Young Werther*, a novel that raised enormous interest in the whole of Europe (Napoleon himself read it seven times and possessed a profound understanding of the work).

The inevitable conclusion is that Werther, the tormented young lover, succumbs to those emotions and passions, but Wilhelm, on the contrary, does not allow himself to be dragged by his passion into self-destruction. Rather, his experiences give rise to self-restraint, and eventually, to wisdom. So that Wilhelm, by end of the trilogy, is Meister – Teacher.

In some way, the characters of Wilhelm and Werther are metaphors for two opposing tendencies in modern Europe: Wilhelm as the struggle for life and constructing a new world; and Werther as submission to pure nihilism.

"Goethe", and here again I quote Abu Bakr Rieger, "recognised the clear and spontaneous core of all genuine Islamic education and the doctrine of Unity," and "...he concludes with the knowledge that only in the meeting with Islam can a person achieve real recognition of the spiritual level that he himself has achieved."

Shaykh Abdalqadir published a *fatwa* in Weimar in 1995 declaring our acceptance of Goethe as a Muslim. At the end of that document he concludes:

"Thus it can be clearly accepted that Europe's greatest poet, and the glory of the German language and intellectual life, is also the first of the Muslims in modern Europe, reawakening in the hearts of people desire for knowledge of God and His Messenger, a knowledge that had lain dormant since darkness had descended on Islamic Spain. In the light of his dazzling confirmation of the Prophet, may Allah bless him and give him peace, he should be known among Muslims as Muhammad Johann Wolfgang Goethe."

The Collaborative Couple[1]
Shaykh Dr. Abdalqadir as-Sufi

I took the title of "The Collaborative Couple" being moved by where in Qur'an, Allah, telling of people entering into the "garden" says, *"They will come singly and in couples."* I felt this contained a great insight for us, if we were to take benefit from it.

I want to, therefore, share with you a view of how things are, in order to arrive at the importance of this vision of the couple as a spiritual entity. Given the nature of present day society and given the intellectual framework and training from which people today come, it can be said that from wherever they emerged they have been given the same grid of training. They, therefore, have the same way of thinking.

I want to preface what I want to say by reminding you that we are not living in a time where everything is business as usual. Anyone who imagines that what has been in place the last twenty-five years is somehow going to go whirling on is profoundly mistaken. We are at the end of a large cycle of time. There is no doubt that the whole intellectual foundation on which this appalling century has existed is already over and swept away. You have to understand the foundation and the

---

[1] A lecture delivered by Shaykh Abdalqadir in 1990 at the University of Malaya, Malaysia.

tactical methodology of what emerges at one level as academic study, has been devalued, smashed, and is over. The last people to know it are the very people producing the thesis and viewpoints based on the dialectical methods of western thinking of the last hundred years.

We can say that the human condition today is on the eve of the world state and that we are already living in a post-literate society. You must understand this and not have any illusions because you are literate and are used to what you call a methodological approach. You are ensconced in a safe society in which you have a role to play. The modern world has already come to political decisions concerning the future, that is, to dethrone literacy for the masses. The basic element of communication for modern people in the coming century will be computer communication. By this I mean the most primitive game systems available to the masses, such as videos, mass films, cartoons, mechanistic music, pop, rock and electronics, without any spiritual or imaginative content. The dominant world of communications in the century ahead will be comic strip books. This is not some futuristic analysis, this is a given of modern urban society.

In Japan last year 60% of published literature was in comic form and, in an international seminar, it was declared openly that this would not be good enough. They would not be satisfied until this 40% of printed matter was radically reduced. Not only that, but their ideologist proposed that it was essential that no one make the claim that "a literate society was superior to an image reading society". The product of this new post-literate society is a valiumised mass creature.

This new society will have five aspects. We are not talking of futurism, but of the condition of modern man.

The first feature of the mass creature is that he is programmable. He will receive social instruction for behaviour and act accordingly. An example is the deliberate programming of black youth in the black ghettos of America with breakdancing, just prior to what was going to be a very dangerous summer of riots. This was a conscious, deliberate, political act to divert the social discontent of the black community.

Secondly, they will be non-alienated. In other words, they will be incapable of questioning, in an active conscious process, that to which they are submitted. They will not do what Socrates did which is, when faced with a moral position, examine it dynamically to find out if it is actually its opposite. Moral science will therefore be eliminated.

Thirdly, they will be outer directed. Social programmation will be so strong, both at work and in play, that no zone of interiority will be possible. Should interiorising emerge, it will be treated by chemical medication where possible.

Fourthly, the mass creature will be non-disruptive and trained to be socially amenable. One model of this is the sort of social exchange that happens in a hotel or on board an aeroplane with everything being 'alright'. The famous expression of 'no problem'.

Fifthly, they will be system submissive. When, in order to allay or offset social changes or crises, they are put into a new systemisation, the mass creature will submit to the new programmation. If they are told they must accept multi-culturalism, then multi-culturalism will become part of their viewpoint. Whatever is offered to them, even as a dialectic issue of excitement and debate, they will submit to it.

In this mass creature any negative response in its program will imply malfunction. Any questioning of society will therefore be defined criminally or medically. Mass passivisation implies a small oligarchy. It cannot be that everyone is being tranquillised if there is no-one to administer it, if there is no tranquillisor. Therefore, we have to identify that there is an élite; not a secret élite, nor a conspiratorial élite, but simply a power élite whose natural function is to assure the non-interference of the masses and their continued exploitation, perpetuating the theft of the world's wealth and human resources.

The social reality of this time can be defined by a very interesting metaphor. The great genius and German conductor Herbert von Karajan died this year (1990) and we have Sony, the great Japanese corporation. There is a link between these two. Karajan was in himself a dynamic, vast, powerful, spiritual being. His conducting of classical music was an event of absolute significance! He embodied, as an empowered individual, the use of the expression of the great composers (Beethoven, Strauss, Bach, Mozart) and it became, in some very personal way, his own expression. You heard Mozart but you saw before you a man to whom this was his expression. The quality of the man was manifested in how he managed his orchestra — he was a whirlwind of power. He brooked no opposition or resistance from the ordinarily gifted musicians as they produced a sound that they themselves had never heard. He lifted them up to another dimension of consciousness. All who played for him confirmed they had newer played like that before and they had never heard the music until that time.

Von Karajan lived at a cross-over period in history and, during the last years of his life, Sony asked him to embody and encapsulate the act of his conducting on a high quality video film. They would film the conducting of music and he would supervise every single detail of the product, but the finished product would be, in fact, a mechanical reproduction of a live event.

Before he died Von Karajan had made a series of videos of all the great pieces of music which he had conducted. At the end of his life Sony, who had taken the contract, had in their possession recordings of Karajan conducting his glorious orchestra. It was no longer Karajan but a mechanical reproduction of him. During the last year of his life Sony approached him and said, "We need not stop here". They showed him in his house in Salzburg, a string quartet playing Schoenberg which was not there. It was a holograph. They said, "We're not finished, we'll start to do it holographically and we'll have the whole Berlin philharmonic orchestra in our living room."

So we move from Karajan to Sony. At the point when Karajan died, Sony had become the master of the world of communication but there was no longer a Karajan to conduct the orchestra. Now the whole musical world admits that if it wanted to conduct music with that intensity of spiritual insight there no longer exists a conductor to do so. The age of the small democratised human being had emerged. This remarkable age of the individualist giant, good or bad, whatever assessment you make of him, was over.

We must see and think beyond the systemic method. The systemic method consists of three strands. The first is structuralist thinking, that you think in structures. The second is the dialectical method — that is, the dynamic of your thinking is through a dialectical process. This is in itself devastatingly obvious and simple as it perpetuates itself by guaranteeing an onward movement which introduces new material, i.e., thesis, antithesis and synthesis, and this creates this new element taken from both sides of the argument. The dialectical method, as we know, has sustained all political discussion. It has sustained itself by creating an illusion of change. What has been presented as a dialectic of right versus left, part of which tore your country to pieces and reformed it, has in our time handed it over to international monetarist forces that control it today. The dialectic between right and left, east and west, can now be seen as completely spurious as the new forces that have emerged indicate unity of the Marxist and the monetarist.

The third is 'objectivity' which is considered to be scientifically superior to all other forms of thinking, and which has been revealed to be precisely this 'myth'. It implies that, in human experience, you can look out there and analyse the other or the object, that you can take it to pieces and examine it, that you can be the sociological observer. Underlying this deception is the encoding of materialist slavery as idealism. As Goethe said, "It is impossible to think of nature as system, nature is life."

The total dismantling of the current disastrous education method is not an intellectual problem. What is necessary is a new way of seeing connected to the life energies of feeling and loving. If we are to address this matter we must unlock the prison of contemporary structuralism. If we decode the structuralist state mechanism, we find that it is not dependent on the sum of its parts or a key part, but on its control of the inner frame of personal living, i.e., the family. The modern state, which is intrinsic tyranny, is totally antipathetic to the human condition and its freedom. It is, in fact, dependent on control and annexation of the family itself.

The modern social model is evolving at present into super states. Europe is the most successful of these new social models in moving logically to a world state which has been ideologically declared since the time of the French revolution. Alongside the super states will be currencies without any numeric value, moving to super currencies, terminating with world currencies, which money itself will be replaced by computerised numerology. Money will be reduced to small change tokens and the world masses to debt enslavement. All this is held in place, not by Interpol, nor by police computers, but by control of the basic human model, the family, through the ancient and simple pattern of the slave state called liberal democracy. We have arrived at the institutionalisation of the incest drama. The Oedipal model.

In the modern state the emergent child fixes on the mother a projected connection which cannot be realised by the lower centres. As the lower centres of sexuality develop the taboo takes its place. Due to the nature of family existence we live today, the child projects on to the mother in the affective sphere, a connection which inhibits the transference into the adult state. In other words, the emergent male fails to see the other. Because the emergent male is able to continue in an affective relationship with the mother, held within the highest sphere of consciousness, denied expression on the sexual level, which is instinctively what he reaches for, he is bound in a frustrated relationship of life which has in it a quality that no other relationship can have during his whole lifetime. Never being fulfilled contains in it a yearning, longing and exultation not touched by anything else in life and making impossible the encounter with the other. The encounter with the other never happens because the separation between the mother and child has not taken place. Instead of transference into the adult state which implies the other, with the woman as partner, a short circuiting of this energy takes place, preferring the ideal bonding back to the mother. This ideal life is a dream life or fantasy life of man with the perfect or ideal woman but still connected at the emotional level with the mother. The angst of separation is avoided and the present is deferred to a dream future. The man emerges into maturity never having, in the affective sphere, broken with the mother. The male, therefore never meets the woman whom he will take as his wife as a partner. As you know, in many cases, the minute the child is born, he will begin to call the wife 'mother'.

The state institutionalises the Oedipal conflict by constructing a rigid frame, a stasis, which leads to a neurotic condition that proposes an ideal of developed, mature, reality that will take place in the future. This ideal condition proffered by the politicians, must be deferred because everything is in chaos and therefore they say we are going to give you the ideal state after the five year plan, after we've dealt with the problem. All the while you are passive, not dealing with the essential problems. The state is dealing with them. Man has no project except inside the family. His whole project is like the wasp in honey, trapped in the yearning, never to be fulfilled, emotional relationship that it can never have. It must end with the man punishing the woman for not being the mother. This is not some neurotic condition, this is the basic condition of modern society today. The proof of it is that you cannot have a modern state unless you have social workers for the poor and psychiatrists for the rich. The ideal state is thus future happiness or infantile bliss. A bliss union with the incestuous partner. Liberté decodes to be license for the incestuous event. Personal undefined freedom is the gift of the state but its price is social slavery. Fraternité becomes the denial of the other, its opposite, and assures the non-emergence of the mature independent woman. The denial of the other is balanced by a mental brotherhood which assures you no one is different. Égalité means there is no parental authority. Laius, the father of Oedipus, is murdered. Louis the sixteenth is beheaded, Ceausescu is taken out and shot. Incest equalises.

The dynamic of the totalitarian state is the stasis of usury, of interest debt. The totalitarian state of which we are members is one which does not permit freedom of expression because it cannot allow this matter to be examined. Interest debt serves the function of the delayed encounter with reality, the inevitable guilt of breaking the incest taboo. It expresses itself as fear of having to pay for it. Incest is the luxury you have to pay for but it is deferred payment. A deferred debt economy assures the postponement of facing up to the cost because there is no neurosis without a guilt. And the guilt method of the totalitarian state is the usury system, which gives you everything you want but you pay for it later. This is causing the death of millions of people in Africa, Asia and South America and not one man anywhere is standing up and saying it should not happen. This is why we come to the "Collaborative Couple", because perhaps the man cannot unless the woman stands by him to say it.

Thus the idealism of state power and its futurist programs, never realised enrichment and success, is incest based, projected fantasy, and an unrealisable future. Idealism sanctions the presence of tyranny and totalitarian status. Idealism is simply inverted materialism and licensed personal gratification. As D.H. Lawrence said, "Incest is the logical foundation of idealism." And I would add idealism is the doctrine of the political democracy. Thus, the minister of education implies the politicisation of knowledge and, therefore, the legalisation of the repressive mechanism and the inevitable censorship of free thinking, which is necessary for the free project would lead to the unmasking of repression and the tyranny that is liberal democracy.

The freedom of just a small group of humans is today rendered almost impossible. This implies the need for a transvaluation of all values. We have to see the movement of the coming century as it was expressed by Nietzsche, who was the greatest philosopher of the last century, speaking, as he said, not for the people of his time but for the people of the future. He indicated the move from the mass man to a bridge that would make it possible for the man, for the woman, the human creature, to emerge.

The only dynamic response to a pachinko palace mass society controlled by a structured information system is a re-educated society which is project orientated, active and collaborative. The non-Oedipal man, that is the differentiated man, will place his life project above his personal life. Do you see what I am saying? As long as man considers his project as earning a living in this enslaved system from which he cannot escape and therefore never comes out of the family system, he is only punishing and destroying his wife, he is destroying the human situation in its totality. As long as he remains inside this trap he is not a man. He is not a man until his project for life is a higher purpose than his own family gratification. As long as family gratification, which is in its basis incestuous, is his foundation, the woman will be the victim. Until a man is prepared to get up and fight for something higher and nobler (and not for himself in selfishness), women will be the victim. This implies a still centre to the human creature, male and female, concerned with meaning and divine knowledge.

Do not think for one minute Islam is in this country. It is not here by 'shari'ah', by 'tariqah' or 'haqiqah'. If it were, you would not have idol worshippers in this country, you would not have women in the condition they are in, and you would not have usury in downtown Kuala Lumpur.

The non-Oedipal, that is the non-collusive woman, will dwell in the growth of her feeling life. This is the non-projective being present in her seeing, touching and hearing centres. Not 'nerve feelings' but the deep seeing and touching and hearing whose expression is ascetic, is beauty (both inwardly and outwardly) and compassion. This is the power, light and force of woman without which the man cannot reach to his higher aspiration. It is this that is short circuited in the bourgeois family. So that all that is left to the woman is 'nerve based' feelings. The reality of the woman touching the petal of the flower; in seeing the light on the water; in hearing the song of the bird, is itself transcendent luminous being. And without it man cannot understand life. He will invent an atom bomb and not have any qualms. He will drop it and not another man will say a word. But if he was with that woman, she would say, "If you make this bomb, what will happen to the child in my womb." That compassion that is exchanged cannot take place because she is busy crying and has locked the door. And he is saying, "What's the matter?"

The otherness of woman is based on her ruling in her feeling life and refusing to cross over into thinking dialectical idealism or refusing to become a pseudo male, that is a political woman. As Wagner said, "The political woman is even worse than the political man, because it is even more against nature." The child's growth will be removed from the imposition of adult connection in its emergent phase. In other words, the child will not be given this projected emotional higher adult feeling from the mother because her adult feeling life will be attuned to her husband. She will be nurturing her husband, not only her child alone. But she will be nurturing her husband with her higher self. This gives the husband the courage for the higher project which is the establishment of justice, equality and the higher values of life. This is best expressed by an old Iraqi lady, a great spiritual strength, who was in our community in Norwich. She saw one of the woman with a child that had started to cry after the mother had fed it. The mother was saying, "What's the matter? Oh, there, there." And the child screamed more. The Iraqi lady could not stand it any more so she got up and took the child from the mother and dumped it on the ground. The child immediately stopped crying. She said, "You had your milk, now on the ground — finished!" She turned to the mother and said, Your job is finished, nothing more to do, let him be."

Like D.H. Lawrence said, "Please! I beg of you, don't love your children." Of course he did not mean in the deep, deep sense. He meant do not do this modern thing about having feelings, where in the end you tyrannise and destroy your children. Now, not all women desire this open condition and not all men are naturally in the wild state of true freedom. The selection of the partner is a prior condition to collaborative freedom. There must be a conscious selection of the partner before this evolved condition can take place. It cannot be based on the extended Oedipal drive, on the copy partner. In other words, if the man simply goes to the woman in this somnambulistic condition, he will simply be looking for the image of the mother.

The superior collaborative woman will require the social freedom of the multiple wife family in order to carry out her higher spiritual task. The superior collaborative man will require the multiple wife family as a human and open non-Oedipal base for the next generation.

The dialectic of adultery, guilt and growing apart, of misogynistic monogamy will end. Monogamy in its nature is misogynistic. As Jane Arden, an English writer and feminist said, "The definition and nature of adultery is, 'It's no fun unless you're cheating on mom.'" In other words, the nature of adultery is that the wife is transformed into the mother and the man is the adolescent going off for an adventure. He comes home, "Where have you been?" "Out!" "What did you do?" "Nothing!" Have no illusion. This is, of course, as common in the Muslim countries as it is in the Kafir ones.

The creation of a community (*jama'a*), and I don't mean in the general sense, but in the intimate, responsible sense, is the basis of a post-statist society. The establishment of an on-the-ground clinic used by its members and a new educational method which preserves the spontaneity of the young for all their lives is necessary.

The modern state is a high security prison. The wardens are fellow prisoners in it. The prison is not locked and yet nobody tries to escape. Why does nobody want to be free? This is a question I have asked for many, many years. And the unravelling of the puzzle reaches to the fundamental pieces of the human identity and beyond the myth of history. It is not difficult to show the way out is through the door. The issue is whether or not the prisoners can recover the power and wildness to make the leap to freedom.

As Salamu Alaikum

The Essentials of Classical Paideia
in the Development of
a Transformative Educational Model[1]
Uthman Ibrahim-Morrison

بِسْمِ اللَّهِ الرَّحْمَنِ الرَّحِيمِ

وَالتِّينِ وَالزَّيْتُونِ ۝ وَطُورِ سِينِينَ ۝ وَهَذَا الْبَلَدِ الْأَمِينِ ۝ لَقَدْ خَلَقْنَا الْإِنسَانَ فِي أَحْسَنِ تَقْوِيمٍ ۝ ثُمَّ رَدَدْنَاهُ أَسْفَلَ سَافِلِينَ ۝ إِلَّا الَّذِينَ آمَنُوا وَعَمِلُوا الصَّالِحَاتِ فَلَهُمْ أَجْرٌ غَيْرُ مَمْنُونٍ ۝ فَمَا يُكَذِّبُكَ بَعْدُ بِالدِّينِ ۝ أَلَيْسَ اللَّهُ بِأَحْكَمِ الْحَاكِمِينَ ۝

At-Tin – The Fig

In the name of Allah, All-Merciful, Most Merciful, *By the fig and the olive, and Mount Sinai, and this safe land, We created man in the finest mould. Then We reduced him to the lowest of the low, except for those who believe and do right actions: they will have a wage which never fails. What could make you deny the Reckoning after this? Is Allah not the Justest of Judges?*

[1] 4th Annual Seminar on Education, Granada, January 6th 2012

Introduction

Insha'Allah, what I hope to do here, as concisely as possible, is to present a condensed excursion across the landscape of the classical *paideia* that was known to the ancient Greek civilisation. It is inevitable that I will be covering some of the same ground covered by Muhammad Mukhtar in his informative and revealing presentation and can certainly affirm the accuracy of his account.[2] I will follow this with the briefest summary of what I modestly consider to be its essential features. Then finally, as a detailed discussion of implementation would take us far beyond the scope of this short essay, I will conclude with a number of broad recommendations as to the approach we should take in principle to the integration of these essentials into the development of a transformative educational model.

Before entering into the heart of our subject matter it is worth noting that the outstanding German classicist Werner Wilhelm Jaeger (July 30, 1888 – October 9, 1961) is credited with having introduced the designation *paideia* into general circulation as a standard term of reference and we certainly all owe a great debt to his immense scholarship for our descriptive access to the cultural modalities of ancient Greek civilisation, and I have certainly relied upon his work, directly and indirectly, to inform this presentation. What Shaykh Dr. Abdalqadir as-Sufi says about this matter also has an important bearing:

> "All the energy against the *gestalt* of the bourgeois came from Germany and it came in the form of a completely new system of Greek studies. All the great Hellenists up until 1914 were Germans, so that in the chaos and destruction

---

[2] Muhammad Mukhtar Medinilla, "Islamic Education versus Assimilation", see p.114

of 1945 while Europe was lifting broken brick from broken brick, the people who ran the new social structure of Europe, placed in chair after chair, favoured in publication house after publication house, the writing on the Greeks was by a new set of technically honoured scholars... We are talking structure, communications, relationships, and political doctrine, so that a bibliography that dates to 1945 will contain German and English scholars, with two or three exceptions. After 1945, that bibliography changes almost completely... In that came the destructuring, or de-struction of the total view of the Greeks, as if systematically they were to remove, stone by stone, the stones of the Acropolis, and to re-evaluate their once profound evaluation. In other words, they made it so there was no way back, and no guides with which to go forward."

Paideia

Properly equipped, let us come to grips then with the ancient Greek notion of *paideia* (παιδεία). What I would recommend at this stage is that we put aside, at least temporarily, the word 'education' with all of its connotations of mass state schooling, national curricula and the endless proliferation of 'courses' and paper qualifications, and focus on the concepts of 'upbringing', which speaks very clearly for itself, and 'culture' not as an anthropological artefact, but rather in the active sense conveyed by its Latin root which signifies to 'cultivate', to 'grow' or to 'tend'. Therefore, bearing in mind its derivation from the word *pais* meaning child, let us think of *paideia* then in general terms as the combination of nurturing practices and learning environments within which a community purposefully carries out the upbringing of its children so that they should grow to embody the desired behaviour, outlook, abilities and traits of character that are presumed to be attainable given sufficient exposure to cultivation. Of course, as Shaykh Abdalqadir has warned, much rests on the basic condition in which the child presents itself:

> "It is inescapable that there must be a whole human being and before you can give it this education that we were looking at earlier, with the Greeks, you need the basic material of a conscious person."

Therefore, in terms of classical *paideia*, we will have to examine the ancient Homeric notions of *areté* and *aidos*; how these manifested in the Spartans and then the various phases of Athenian development to culminate in the Hellenistic expression which spread out beyond Greece to Rome, Alexandria and the Muslim world to become the basis of the classical humanistic education we associate with the Renaissance and which remained the basic template for scholarship amongst the aristocracy and the gentry throughout the middle ages and well into the early modern period – even surviving in somewhat attenuated form into the 20th century in the English public schools where certain 'Homeric' qualities fed the roots of what was considered the ideal of gentlemanly conduct – I remind you of the account I gave last year concerning the Etonian explorer, writer and photographer, the late Sir Wilfred Thesiger (1910 – 2003) and Abdalhaqq Bewley's summary of the essentials of this ethos as expressed by Dr. Thomas Arnold, whose reforms laid the foundations for the English public school system:

> "If my boys have four things when they leave school I

consider I have done my duty by them. Those four things are piety, loyalty, generosity and courage."

I will come to *aidos* (αἰδώς) first which, though it cannot be entirely separated from *areté* (ἀρετή), can be summed up fairly straightforwardly as the overriding driving force behind the best behaviour and good actions, which the individual experiences morally as an inner concern for what is owed to the gods, concern for the fulfilment of one's obligations to one's fellow men and concern for that which is due to oneself. Furthermore, because of the close association in the Greek mind between moral qualities, bodily symmetry and physical prowess, aidos could also be said to encompass these attributes and to underlie the enduring ideal of the man both beautiful and good (*kalos kagathos* – καλὸς κἀγαθός). The explanation of *areté* is not quite so simple.

The quality of *areté* was central to the ancient Greek ideal of manly excellence and defines the attribute with which the epic homeric heroes were so abundantly endowed. In English the word 'virtue' is most frequently used to convey this quality, but not altogether adequately since *areté* was wider in that it encompassed a range of accomplishments that exceeded the scope covered by 'virtue', whilst 'virtue' itself implies a brand of morality not easily accommodated within the domain of *areté*. A useful description as to what it meant for the Greeks is that:

"... *areté* was that peculiar excellence that makes a thing, or a horse, or a soldier, or a hero, the best, the most effective, of their kind." (Castle)

The fact of the matter is that over the period of roughly a millennium from the Homeric era to the mature Hellenism of classical Athens, the Greek ideal of *areté* underwent a number of shifts determined by whatever criteria of excellence happened to be in the ascendant at any given time. Therefore, pivotal to its expression in Homer's heroes was personal honour, which would have included prowess in battle, the pursuit of mental as well as physical superiority over one's peers, and that one's superior mettle should be witnessed in full public view. By the time we come to Sparta at her height, the key to *areté* had shifted from an emphasis on the achievement of great deeds purely for the enhancement of one's personal standing, to a willingness to fight and die for the preservation of the polis, one's city-state. This then became the standard for the whole of Greece. Shaykh Abdalqadir's observations here are revealing:

> "The Spartan model was a state model in the most extreme form in which the education of the child was totally seconded to the vision of the state. So intense is this that our reading of Plato's *Republic* seems simply like an essay on Spartan education, and of course remember that it was not just in Sparta, but sometimes also in Athens, that if a child was not healthy they flung it over a cliff. There would be a significant reduction in modern European populations if this happened. I am not saying it is good or bad." (Achilleus)

Therefore, Plato's definition of *paideia* in *The Laws* (Νόμοι) comes as no surprise, it is:

> "The education in *areté* from youth onwards, which makes men passionately desire to become perfect citizens, knowing both how to rule and how to be ruled on a basis of justice." (Castle)

Jaeger states the matter as follows:

> [Tyrtaeus (Sparta's great lyric poet)]... "has recast the Homeric ideal of the single champion's *areté* into the *areté* of the patriot and with that new faith he strives to inspire his whole society. He is endeavouring to create a nation of heroes... he who falls among the foremost fighters and loses his dear life in winning glory for his city... though he is beneath the earth he becomes immortal." (Jaeger)

By the middle of the 5th century BC Athens, which had long since gained ascendancy over Sparta as the leaders of the Hellenic world, had become a prosperous, bourgeois society. The old ideals which had placed the highest premium on devotion to civic duty, gave way in the minds of ambitious young men to personal advancement in the pursuit of a political career:

> "The new ideal of political *areté* had been born: no longer valour, or service to the state; personal political leadership, the management of other men, was the *areté* of the new Athenian." (Castle)

This development coincided with the advent of the leading sophists such as Protagoras, Gorgias and Isocrates, whose pragmatic approach to the questions of virtue and wisdom stood at odds with the likes of Plato and Aristotle who took their guidance from a previous age. Hence, Plato in the eponymously titled dialogue *Protagoras* (Πρωταγόρας), has the protagonist deliver a rather facile definition of *areté* as:

> "... the proper care of one's personal affairs, so as best to manage one's own household, and also of the state's affairs, so as to become a real power in the city, both as a speaker and man of action."

This, of course, already begins to sound uncomfortably familiar to our sensitive ears, even though modern representative democracy as we know it bears little resemblance to the direct forms of democracy practised by the Athenians. Therefore, we come to the final phase of Greek education in *areté*, which under the influence of the sophists had become what we have come to think of as Hellenistic (in other words the culture had transcended its original racial, tribal and geographical limitations) and by the time of Aristotle (384 – 322 BC) had reached its mature form which would remain more or less unchanged for centuries. *Paideia*, rather than being the active means to an end had become the static end in itself – the 'culture' called Hellenism.

Given all of these generally degenerative changes in emphasis over the period in question, it almost goes without saying that the methods and modalities employed in order to achieve the desired results will also have been subject to variation according to time and circumstance. However, as we wish to proceed to identify the essentials of classical *paideia*, it will not be necessary to go into great detail here. As I have already mentioned, the Spartan model was determined by the strict requirements of the state and more or less reduced the city to an enormous barracks where the purpose from the age of seven onwards, was to engender the obedient capacity to endure extremes of pain and discomfort as preparation for the achievement of the one supreme goal: conspicuous physical courage and victory on the field of battle.

The Athenians, on the other hand, sought to cultivate an all-round excellence based on an ideal balance between the physical, intellectual, aesthetic and moral dimensions of the individual. Private schools were already flourishing by the 5th century BC where physical education and 'music' (which included literary instruction and arithmetic) were the staple fare for most boys between the ages of seven and fourteen. The sons of the privileged classes would then be taken on by their elders, introduced to the functions of civic life and be expected to learn the laws and functions of the city's cultural and governing institutions. With the arrival of the sophists (4th BC) there came a significant shift of emphasis from learning through practising a way of life to learning through the medium of words, and at secondary level (for those who could afford it) the technical demands of a political vocation led to the rise of training in oratory through the teaching of rhetoric, philosophy and classical literature (alongside the usual physical education); arithmetic, geometry, astronomy and music theory occupied a subordinate place, nevertheless, one can clearly identify the foundations for the mediaeval *trivium* (grammar, dialectic, rhetoric) and *quadrivium* (geometry, arithmetic, astronomy, music theory). It is also worth mentioning here that by this stage the admission of girls to both elementary and secondary schools was commonplace.

Recovering the Essentials

Having completed this brief survey of the practice of *paideia* amongst the ancient Greeks, there can be no doubt about the richness and depth of this immense heritage which the spread of the Alexandrian eruption, the impact of the Roman empire and ultimately the light of al-Andalus, have bequeathed to western history and philosophy. However, modern education no longer provides access to this rich inheritance, on the contrary, it has concealed it. This point was succinctly made by my esteemed colleague Sidi Muhammad Mukhtar in his excellent essay "Islamic Education versus Assimilation"[3] where he warns:

> "A widespread misconception nowadays is the idea of the unassailable heights attained by the ancient city-states. Our excuse for doing what we do is because that is how it used to be with the ancient Greeks. However, their state completely avoided this utilitarianism, which consists of accepting culture only insofar as it benefits the state and being rid of anything that serves no obvious purpose." (Medinilla)

Before proceeding it is also necessary at this point to remind ourselves of Shaykh Abdalqadir's summation of what is certainly the most disturbing challenge we now face. He says:

> "... we have returned to the original idea of a Platonic *paideia*, yet we have already seen that the imprinting of the technical society has paralysed men and women – men much more than women. So that the most that it would look as if we can hope for from the adult of today, in extremis, would be their intellectual confirmation of what I am saying and a psychotic inability to relate it to their own lives..." (*The Shield of Achilleus*)

Therefore, it is important that we accept that the effective recovery of this legacy now depends upon the determination of the parents, teachers and leaders of the new Muslim communities of Europe, who have realised its vital importance in preparing the soil for the deepest penetration of the roots of the *deen* into

---

[3] p.114

The Essentials of Classical Paideia

these lands and that this will not be achieved without personal submission to a regenerative *paideia* conspicuously imbued with the recuperative remedy of *tasawwuf*.

On the basis of the present examination of *paideia* as it was experienced by the ancient Greeks, it is my view that the essentials of the classical picture may be reduced to the following five points:

1. The Greeks regarded education as the process of rearing children to become good men and women; they did not succumb to the doctrine that the main priority was instruction in the making of things or preparation for earning a living. They were the first to see education as the means of shaping human character in conformity to an ideal.

2. Physical education remains a constant whatever other changes may have occurred. For the Greeks this was centred upon the disciplines of the *palaestra* (wrestling) and the *gymnasium* (athletics). This was competitive in nature and focused upon the development of strength, endurance, agility and courage. The other key element here was dance, which emphasised all-round command of physical movement and a balanced development of the whole body.

3. The primacy of music. Shaykh Dr. Abdalqadir expresses this in the following emphatic and unambiguous terms:

> "The Platonic *paideia*, the Platonic spiritual education, considered that its essential was music, so that the creation of a free man would mean the science of music, the art of music, the expression of music, and the listening to music. Alongside this Plato put another art which was the dance, and it was not the dance in the decadent sense of classical ballet, it was the dance of the body, normal, ordinary, joyful." (*The Shield of Achilleus*)

However, given the commercialised debasement of the modern day musical environment, I would only add to this the caveat that the purposes of musical education were aesthetic, ennobling and spiritual, and intended to produce a refined *amateur* (with the emphasis on love) rather than a professional performer. I would also add that a secondary function of the Athenian music schools was instruction in mathematics and geometry.

4. Classical literature and especially poetry were essential as the medium through which the highest aspirations towards uprightness of character and nobility of conduct (as well as warning and admonition), were proclaimed, publicised and preserved. These would be committed to memory, sung and recited. This also ensured access to the historical narrative essential for the affirmation of cultural identity and grounding of the science of politics.

5. Plato's vision of education for the élite considered as essential the discipline of philosophy for the acquisition of the wisdom required to master the self and to integrate the various human faculties into a harmonious whole.

Conclusion

The task of integrating these elements into the development of a transformative educational model, of course, rests with our communities – the parents, the teachers and the leaders striving together, although it must always be understood that parental responsibility comes first, and that therefore, the activation of the parental sense of urgency is paramount.

As for the teachers, if we wish to recover the essentials of classical *paideia*, then we must remember that its primary aim was the raising of excellent men and women, therefore as parents we must insist on excellence of character as the first qualification of those who will teach our children (bearing in mind that their training will first have begun in the home). The responsible Greek father of old who possessed the means, did not simply send his offspring to 'school', he sent them to a teacher or teachers – this is a crucial distinction because what was being sought was a direct transmission based upon personal reputation – and for good measure, in the case of a child being sent to a school he would be accompanied by a *paidagōgos* (παιδαγωγός). The *paidagōgos* (from which we derive the term pedagogue) was a trusted member of the parental household, usually a slave or *mawla*, who apart from providing physical protection was also expected to:

> "... supervise his young charge's manners in the home and in the street and even in school, where he sat in attendance as a symbol of paternal authority throughout the school day. This moral supervision by the *paidagōgos* must be stressed. He was more important than the schoolmaster, because the latter only taught a boy his letters, but the *paidagōgos* taught him how to behave, a much more important matter in the eyes of his parents." (Castle)

I mention this not to undermine the standing of the teacher, on the contrary, it is to underline firstly the primacy of the home in terms of setting standards and secondly, our expectation that the teacher's own personal example will reinforce and improve upon the family training, thereby dispensing with any need for the Greek style 'pedagogue'. To emphasise further still the crucial nature of the personal nexus between the teacher and the pupil, I am pleased once again to be able to repeat the observations of Muhammad Mukhtar, who states:

"I am not speaking about scholastic education nor, much less, about creating an academic caste. I am speaking only of looking for the right form, of finding a way, in this time and place, to develop our own educational model; one that will allow us in the near future to establish the *ijaza*, the personal accreditation between the pupil and the teacher; not between the student and the institution. An *ijaza* is the certificate by which the teacher recognises and authorises his pupil to exercise or teach a certain discipline. We must establish a flexible organisation, adapted to the rhythms of learning and to the growth of every individual learner. We must recover traditional teaching methods..." (Medinilla)

To conclude finally, what is required is a community of teachers and students. What I mean by this is a setting in which the organic as well as the organised exchange by means of which the dynamic of transmission, inspiration and guidance between teachers and students is intended to flourish. Schools as we know them represent the very antithesis of what is required. Therefore, the setting for our renewal of *paideia* that is not a genuine community in itself must be situated at the heart of a thriving civic environment, without unnecessary separation from its multifarious human rhythms and realities. We too, like the ancient Greeks, have our *areté*, one that is sustained not by the conception of a poetical ideal, but by the love for one whose human perfection and whose deeds ﷺ are a match for the genius of ancient myth, while being firmly rooted in recorded history. Abdalhaqq Bewley in his memorable essay "Muslim Identity in the Present Age", has indicated what we can expect for the best of our young people:

"They will truly be noble youths following the very highest aspect of the sunna of the Prophet ﷺ by truly embodying those noblest qualities of character – *taqwa*, sincerity, truthfulness, generosity, courage, modesty, patience, forbearance, and complete trustworthiness – which he himself exemplified and which he only came to perfect. This is what education sets out to achieve; this is *futuwwa*, the chivalric ethos that, as Shaykh Abdalqadir makes clear, lies at the heart of every true manifestation of Allah's *deen* and is necessary for its re-establishment in every age. And among them will be those who take on the quest of the Grail, whose reality is in fact nothing other than direct experience of the Divine Presence, those who set out and win through to the supreme goal of all human endeavour, the vision of the Face of their Lord."

We rely upon our leaders therefore to hold this reminder in their hearts with a vision and inspiration equal to that of the poets of antiquity and to marshal the necessary people and resources to create the environment most conducive to our success. *La hawla wa la quwwata ila billahi l-'alliyi l-'adheem.*

Sources

The Noble Qur'an: A New Rendering of its Meanings in English by Abdalhaqq & Aisha Bewley
Paideia, the Ideals of Greek Culture by W. Jaeger
The Shield of Achilleus by Shaykh Dr. Abdalqadir as-Sufi
Ancient Education and Today by E.B. Castle
"Islamic Education versus Assimilation" by Muhammad Mukhtar Medinilla. p.114 of this volume.

"Muslim Identity in the Present Age" by Abdalhaqq Bewley
"Myth, Narrative and History (Part II)" by Uthman Ibrahim-Morrison and Abdassamad Clarke

For Whom the Bell Tolls
The Trojan Horse[1] Autopsy Toolkit

Uthman Ibrahim-Morrison
Ibrahim Lawson
Jakob Werdelin
Abdassamad Clarke

Abstract

If, as more than one well-informed Muslim educationalist has affirmed, the Muslim teachers at the core of the Birmingham schools 'Trojan Horse' conspiracy are "guilty as charged", then this document serves to elucidate that their guilt is in fact of a very different nature from that in the charge, and that the Trojans and the Greeks in our metaphor are not at all whom we assume them to be. The real starting point of the essay that follows is thus the passage in which we take seriously the metaphor of the Trojan Horse and, in so doing, come to an entirely different perspective, that the Trojans are the ordinary men and women of the United Kingdom and the Trojan Horse is the various ways the political class inveigles them into

[1] Named after the so-called 'Trojan Horse conspiracy' in Birmingham schools in 2013, subsequently itself exposed as a fabrication and a conspiracy.

accepting the state's blandishments and then disenfranchising them when they accept them. Muslim teachers are just the tip of our iceberg, for we are all Trojans, and our guilt is in having accepted the beguiling offer of the state to the right to an education for all its citizens within the frame of the welfare state. Our guilt is in accepting the right to be citizens of a democratic society with a right to pursue our own paths to wellbeing, tolerating others and being in turn tolerated. Our guilt is in believing that one has freedom of expression, for that freedom only belongs to those who express what the political class and media élite consider to be in accord with their own prejudices. Our guilt is in actually believing in British values more than British people themselves do, and certainly more than the political class and media élite do.

Thus, our essay necessarily weaves a number of themes together: the nature of the nation-state and its collapse in our times; the political class and their uneducated posturings and anti-democratic rule by diktat; the nature of knowledge, particularly rational knowledge and enquiry and the ability to think and to question; the way that knowledge, character and the ability to judge complex issues are transmitted through education; and the collapse of education itself resulting in the kind of uneducated responses such as those of the political class, which, alarmingly, are not only irrational but arguably go against the legal basis of our society. That is all merely the symptom of a condition that affects people at every level of our society and is the deep story behind the demise of the state and a short-lived international order that had pertained until comparatively recently. Enlightenment values are disintegrating and in the face of the liberating forces emerging, the intellectually challenged react dictatorially, thus revealing their bankruptcy.

The nub of the essay lies in the section on opening up thinking as questioning. This will come as a surprise to outdated votaries of Enlightenment rationality, otherwise known as 'modernity', who have taken it as rigid dogma unaware of the tremendous upheavals that have taken place in thought and that have opened thinking up to entirely new vistas. It will also come as a surprise to many Muslims tempted by the seeming security of the modern Islamic dogma being forged in our age that holds no water, neither with respect to the traditional perspective nor to the exciting and challenging post-Enlightenment approaches to which Muslims are surprisingly the natural heirs.

The next important part of this essay is the section on the transmission to children of this ability to interrogate issues in a constructive and liberating way, for what is the Western and thus British system of education if not the opening up of the faculties of the student to equip them to be able to hear, see, think and then act in ways that are positive and life-enhancing? This needs reiteration. The political class have in this century overseen the reduction of education – from the kindergarten to the post-graduate, doctoral and professorial levels – to nothing more than equipping people to be servile citizens of the modern state, which is already outmoded, and functionaries to serve the corporate and banking oligarchy, who are even more outmoded. We cite as evidence of the ending of the 'age of finance' the increasing numbers of suicides among high-level bankers and financiers. They know something the populace at large don't.

The paradoxical core of the issue, which is all paradox and in which nothing is what it proclaims itself to be, is that the proclamation of noble 'British values' is being used for precisely the opposite purpose by a self-serving political class intent on servilely carrying out the wishes of an oligarchic financial order that is itself in terminal collapse and bringing the entire global civic order down around our ears. This is certainly not an issue that is confined to UK plc.

The paradoxical outcome of the case will probably be that alert Muslims will awaken to the nature of the deceptively named 'social contract' and begin to establish what they know to be true, but in a more humble and communitarian way. Understanding these tremendous global themes, they will go to work locally but without fanfare. The age is tired of grand rhetoric and wants to see genuine action. In that global understanding, the time has come for intelligent people to abandon useless and outdated façades, such as that of the nation-state, and think globally. In the case of the Muslims they will think of the Umma but when they do so they will also need to remember that the Umma always comprised Muslims, Christians, Jews and a variety of other groupings. If the Muslims take things forward they must do so on behalf of everyone, everywhere.

The Autopsy

Food for Thought or Sound Bites

We are primarily concerned here with understanding the historical forces and dynamics at play in order to offer, not only the beleaguered Muslim community but readers at large, the means to articulate more than just an emotional reaction to the constant stream of press 'revelations', especially since the overriding emotional environment that has been generated by government policy over the last decade has been one of fear. We hope that it will be a useful resource for people who are seeking building blocks solid enough to begin to construct for themselves something more than a transient, superficial, media driven reaction or a sensationalised impression of WHAT IS GOING ON? and WHY THE BIG DEAL? To that end we are taking the unusual step of **highlighting** those items we consider to be significant as **'sound bites'** or **'food for thought'** that will serve as tent pegs so that the delicate intellectual construction work of finding the language and asking the questions that will lead to the emergence of meaningful reflections or a deeply rooted understanding, is less likely to be swept away in the hysterical blizzard of breaking news, investigative speculation, meaningless statistics, the selective parade of bewildered parents, students and assorted locals providing *vox populi* pieces to camera, and the hollow grandstanding of competing politicians and community 'spokespersons'.

We hope this overview will be of some assistance to people wishing to reach a slightly more detached and elevated vantage point from which to get a steady view of the broader picture. This is highly important given that what the Muslims are being subjected to today, others were subjected to yesterday, and yet more will be subjected to tomorrow. Therefore, a detailed forensic examination of the so called 'facts' of the case or of the arguments being traded by politicians and pundits are not our priority. We have fundamental questions to ask, for it is the questions we ask, rather than the answers we get, that will open the way to the thinking and the path to meaning that is crucial.

THE TROJAN HORSE METAPHOR

But before coming to that let us first be clear as to the

significance of the ubiquitous metaphor of the eponymous 'Trojan Horse'. According to the *Concise OED* it is: "something intended to undermine or secretly overthrow an enemy or opponent – *ORIGIN* from the hollow wooden statue of a horse in which a number of Greeks are said to have concealed themselves in order to enter Troy." In other words, it is a well established byword, recovered from the rich and ancient stock of the Homeric European legacy, for a strategic military subterfuge (in this instance taking the form of an impressive tributary offering aimed at the disguised penetration of the enemy's position. Whence the well known admonition: 'Beware of Greeks bearing gifts!') Let us now come to one or two important questions:

Who are the 'Greeks' and what exactly constitutes the 'Trojan Horse' in this drama? In the scenario that we have been fed by way of the 'breaking news' there are several discrete sets of candidates for these central roles: Govt. ministers; schools; parents; students; boards of governors; extremist conspirators; Ofsted. Of course, we are supposed to believe that the extremist Muslim plotters represent 'Greeks' who have conspiratorially infiltrated the Boards of School Governors (Trojan Horses?) in order to take over a number of state schools in Birmingham (or Troy?). The metaphor breaks down instantly, since, according to legend, the Greeks and Trojans had been engaged in a protracted war, finishing up in a lengthy siege. Are we to imagine that the state educational apparatus in Birmingham (Troy?) and across the nation as a whole, has long been at war with and held under siege by Muslim extremists (the Greeks)? Did the Muslim extremists then, true to legend, build the eponymous Trojan Horses (School Boards)? No, they didn't. It is important to understand who did build them because that will identify the Greeks. Well, the so-called extremists actually found these Boards of Governors ready and waiting, which makes them sound much more like the poor old Trojans, does it not?

The Boards of Governors were actually constructed by Central and Local Government, and so we are forced to reinterpret the scenario accordingly, meaning that we are compelled to consider a rather unexpected, but by no means uninteresting reinterpretation: namely, that the state (Greeks) had been engaged in a protracted process of systematic state-formation, which in order to succeed required the complete subjugation of an autonomous, proud and hence intractable and suspicious British population (Trojans) to 'law and order' (progress). Therefore they built for them an entire national school apparatus, with the added incentive of Boards for parent governors – do these not sound more like the Greek gifts (Trojan Horses) we heard about, the ones to be wary of? Therefore, after long years of resistance, the hapless Muslim community of Birmingham (the Trojans) get up one fine morning to find themselves face to face with an entire state school apparatus, complete with Boards of Governors, ready and waiting for them. The most adventurous and enterprising of them decide to climb aboard and get it to work for them only to find themselves surrounded by armed Greek enforcers (Ofsted), there to make it plain that Greeks are not in the habit of giving something for nothing and that they expect to have things done their way, or not at all!

There are more questions to be asked: Are all of these wonderful state facilities set up as traps for the unwary? What are schools for? What are Academies? How 'free' are 'Free Schools'? What lessons does the Trojan Horse legend teach us about how to approach the tempting blandishments of the state?

But, what is the state? These are just some of the questions that are pressing in upon us, so let us turn to the business of questioning.

On Asking Useful Questions

There are two perspectives on this scandal which must be kept separate, initially at least. On the one hand we have what might be thought of as a rational and informed discussion about serious and important issues. On the other hand we have this sort of thing (from the Daily Telegraph, where else?):

> **"Teachers and governors involved in the alleged 'Trojan Horse' Islamic takeover plot face life-long bans from all schools in Britain under new powers being taken by Michael Gove.**
>
> "Mr Gove, the Education Secretary, wants to use the new powers to ensure that anyone found to have been involved in the plot – allegedly designed to Islamise secular state education in Birmingham – is prevented from working in schools elsewhere in the country."

This text would be ideal for use in an introduction to thinking skills lesson, for two reasons. Firstly, the content itself exemplifies the kind of sloppy use of language and reasoning that seems to characterise much of what we read on the internet. How, for example, can someone be involved in an alleged plot? To be involved in something, it has to exist; if it only allegedly exists then you can only be allegedly involved, surely? **Are we to understand that the government is proposing action against people for being allegedly involved in an alleged plot? If that were the case then an allegation would be sufficient as proof; there would be no difference between** the two. Of course, the allegation by itself is enough for the hard of thinking, for whom evidence and argument are merely confusing.

The second paragraph builds on the license established by the first – notice that "the alleged 'Trojan Horse' Islamic takeover plot" has become simply 'the plot – allegedly designed to Islamise secular state school education'. One is reminded of a book on the richly fertile imaginary life of young children entitled, 'Let's Pretend this is a Snake – By the Way it is a Snake'. Now we have graduated to, 'Let's Allege there is a Plot – By the Way, There is a Plot'.

The problem with this kind of deceitful 'logic' is the second reason why it would be useful in a thinking skills lesson: **why do we need to improve our thinking skills? Because once we accept nonsense, we open the door to the kind of dangerous idiocy exemplified in the comments on the article, helpfully also published by the Telegraph:**

> **thecccuuttsman** • 3 days ago: Ban them from schools for life? They should be on "conspiracy to incite terrorism" charges. If these four were Irish & we were living in the 70's they would be looking at 20 years. If I remember correctly wasn't a British citizen sentenced to death just for handing out Christian leaflets or something similar in Pakistan? Surely it's got to be "an eye for an eye" when Muslims in this country are found to be doing what these four were planning.
>
> **Unionjackjackson thecccuuttsman** • 3 days ago: **There's thousands more like them living amongst us**

rugbyboy Unionjackjackson • 3 days ago: Yes, and time to root them out!

moraywatson rugbyboy • 2 days ago: Or, we could properly identify Islam as a political ideology and stop appeasing the bogus "religious" demands of its Muslim adherents.

haphaestus moraywatson • 2 days ago: This is so important. Islam is NOT a religion. Words are important, definitions are important! As long as we can't even call something what it is, we can't win.

London Eye haphaestus • 2 days ago: Correct. Islam is a cult and ideology not a religion per se. It's main objective is conversion of ALL the Worlds infidels and kuffirs by indoctrination and finally, if all else fails by the sword. The Muslim Brotherhood manifesto, which is locked in those secret rooms at the back of all Mosques is quite clear. The conversion of the unenlightened and those following the wrong path, will be at first, by covert indoctrination and the infiltration of our Islamic brothers into positions of authority and power. The rightful path must be taught to ALL regardless of their present or past beliefs. Only Allah's teachings are the way to a complete and fulfilling life on this Earth. So now you know why these radicals kicked out the white heads and put themselves into positions to spread their vile and oppressive ideology!

Bruce Hamilton moraywatson • 2 days ago: I agree. I think of Mohammed as having been a very worldly and ambitious, confused Christian.

pete_marsh moraywatson • 2 days ago: The best definition of Islam I heard was 'an expression of Arab nationalism with some religion thrown in'. It's 90% ideology in the UK, and I have honestly come to believe that it's a bigger threat to Anglo-Celtic culture than Hitler.

the_ferryman pete_marsh • 2 days ago: Main Kampf or the Koran? A tough call.

Phantomsby the_ferryman • a day ago: Mein Koran?

Ethelwulf rugbyboy • 2 days ago: "What you sow shall you reap." And this is exactly what the LibLabCON have been doing these past 40 years. Whatever the Quislings in Britain say, Islam is a THREAT to this nation.

What a rich resource for teachers!
Irony aside, what does all this mean? Is this just par for the course and nothing to be overly concerned about? Or is it the ominous rumblings of an incipient totalitarianism coming soon to a democracy near you? How worried should we be? What should be our response? And who do we mean by 'we'?
People following this scandal may well be reminded of the Salman Rushdie affair where there seemed to be a similar clash between liberal secular values and those of Islam, or some/many/most Muslims at least. It appears to be the same issue and that not only has it never gone away, it has been building inevitably towards further and further conflict. Even if some

kind of temporary compromise is achieved regarding state policy on schooling in the UK – and the issue will inevitably re-surface regarding independent 'faith schools' – the underlying problem has not yet been identified, let alone addressed.

What, then, lies behind this scandal? **Is it an inevitable clash between reason and religion, as many think? Or is it the lack of reason? Could it be the lack of (real) religion? Is it a failure of multiculturalism? Or the result of unchecked xenophobia?** Probing deeper, it might be a consequence of neo-conservatism and the need to manufacture consent, in Chomsky's memorable phrase. **Manufacturing consent for the demonstrably insane policies of the political agenda set by neo-conservatism[2] requires a narrowing of the public debate to simple black and white alternatives, which inevitably creates an 'us and them' narrative and consequently a useful enemy on whom to focus attention.**

It all depends on where you want to set out your stall. **What kind of overall paradigm is the right frame for the Trojan Horse Schools scandal? And here, it might be as well to remember an old adage of social research: a theory can be judged on three criteria – it can be simple, generalisable or true, or any two of these, but never all three. Try it for yourself and you will see.** What it means in this case is that whatever explanation we tend towards in the case of these schools we have three choices, not four. Our explanation will be either:

---

[2] The neo-conservative connection is particularly worrying because of the 'noble lie', a widely misunderstood concept that has demonstrably led to actual lying with disastrous outcomes in recent history. Thus, Michael Gove's engagement in neo-conservatism is deeply troubling.

1. Simple and generalisable to all schools/communities/Muslims/politicians/Ofsted inspections etc; in which case it will be false;

2. Simple and true, in which case specific only to the particular schools/communities/Muslims/politicians/Ofsted inspections etc. and not generalisable (i.e. not a basis for policy);

3. Generalisable and true, but unfortunately not simple (sorry about that).

What will be lacking, if the principle is accurate, is the highly desirable but impossible luxury of an explanation that is true – surely what we all want – simple – so we can all understand it easily, even Telegraph readers et al – and generalisable – so that it can be turned into government policy for use on all similar occasions. Wouldn't it be nice if the world worked like that? If all schools, all communities, all Ofsted inspections, all governments could just agree on and stick to a basic set of undeniably true and easy to understand principles.

To think more deeply about this, we can ask: where did we get such an idea from? Whence this desire for complete and simple explanations? Why do we so often hear the claim that 'it is all very simple...? What is wrong with people that we can't all just agree and get along?' Is that the goal of human civilisation? Are we hoping one day to emerge into the pure light of a utopian rationality where we finally, collectively realise that all life really is simple and easy to understand and explain?

Or is that starting to sound like some kind of ideological requirement? If so, where did this demand for what Wittgenstein calls 'the crystalline purity of logic' come from? Why are we so uncomfortable with the idea of irreducible complexity?

Let us consider the suggestion that communication between two parties always involves an *aporia* or impossible necessity. This is true even in our 'internal' communication with ourselves, i.e. our own personal understanding of anything and everything. An *aporia* (ἀπορῐα) is an unbridgeable gap (Greek: *aporos* – ἄπορος) but more than that, it is a gap that also has to be crossed somehow. What transpires is that all attempts to cross are ultimately provisional. **In terms of linguistic communication, we recognise Plato's observation of the 'weakness of the logos'. But this is an advantageous weakness, a necessary weakness because without it there could be no language at all; and without language, there would be no being, to reference an earlier philosopher, Parmenides of Elea. In other words, without language there would be no human world, no humanity.**

How then does this weakness of the logos constitute the essence of language, of our being human? And conversely, how does the attempt to remove this weakness and discover a final answer to every possible question lead to an inhuman non-world, where, paradoxically, nothing is true and everything is permitted?

These are, of course, philosophical questions and, for serious thinkers, philosophy is the court of ultimate appeal whenever there appears a seemingly irresolvable crisis in the sciences, natural or social. This is important to recognise: philosophy can sit in judgement on scientific truth, but not vice versa. Wisdom is nobody's handmaiden.

Briefly, for there are no simple answers, the meaning of a word, of a text, is porous; there is no one, final and complete meaning and so there is always room for further interpretation. This is partly because language is always meaningful in some context of use, and contexts themselves are uncontainable or boundless. What this entails is a process whereby meaning is always being constructed by the participants in a discourse or exchange of language and this is potentially infinite. What makes a discourse, and language itself, aporetic is that not only is no final and complete meaning ever attainable, but neither can judgement be indefinitely postponed on that count. All acts of communication can therefore be seen to be creative, to introduce new meaning into the world, and thank goodness for that.

This is a higher order consideration and not something which our Telegraph commenters will particularly appreciate. Nor, one imagines will our Ronseal Men at the helm of the ship of the state who would rather that reality be 'exactly as it says on the tin'. But then, this is a feature of political discourse where complexity and nuance are considered signs of weakness and 'flip-flopping'.

This, however, is a cause for hope. **Rudolf Steiner believed that society had three elements that were not only separate but had to be kept apart. The three can be summarised as 'politics', 'economics' and 'spirit'.** The world of the spirit includes everything which is specific to 'internal' human realities and well-being and so extends from health and sanity, to morality, art and spirituality, and, especially, all that is meaningful to us. Politics is the science of power over others and economics the realm of material possessions and all that concerns their acquisition. Clearly, there is a degree of overlap; but **the importance of separation can be seen when we ponder such questions as 'Is there a price on health?' 'Should bankers be able to buy politicians?' 'Can the government** really tell us what to believe?' 'Are politicians to be relied upon to run the finances of the state?' 'What happens when religious scholars are put in charge of society?' and so on.

The conclusion is that we can recognise that politicians today HAVE to take a black and white, simplistic view, that religion and science do not occupy the same space of reason, that greed is an unworthy, and unsustainable, basis for social morality. **We must try to see that everything important in life is and must be endlessly questionable in the positive sense that the obligation to THINK is never discharged and questioning builds the unique path that every single one of us is on individually from birth to death. Of course, this thinking is never merely ratiocination; it is what makes us who we are and we lose sight of this at our peril.**

Cooperative Learning and Critical Thinking for the Classroom

As the Islamist 'Trojan Horse' scandal picked up speed in the media, governmental agencies and political spokespersons vied with each other to present ever more draconian measures to defend the administration of schools from extremist infiltration.

An extremely pertinent question for our educators might be: How do we arm the minds of the children? – for the truth is that the children, not the schools, are the real target. (And remembering, of course, that this arming of the minds must be done without preaching specific versions of faith systems, even that of secularism).

The Norwich Muslim community's interfaith outreach group is in the process of developing a series of RE discovery exercises aimed at primary and secondary schools. We have found that structural Cooperative Learning, being firmly grounded in social constructivism, offers a unique tool to teach learners to cope with opposing viewpoints and provides tools to de-construct messages, discovering and working outwards from their own understanding. **Being told to be critical of certain material presented in the context of a 60 minute lesson is not the same as teaching critical thinking as a life skill – all the more so because critical thinking without a stable vantage point (i.e. argument for argument's sake) is little more than an exercise in nihilistic futility.**

The key to this vantage point is to help learners reflect – at their individual levels – on issues of epistemology ("How do I know something?") and ontology ("What is this world that I am in") in the very practical zone of personal beliefs and experiences in the classroom. The recently published book 21C *Trivium* is recommended reading for those of us in favour of re-invigorating the teaching of logic and rhetoric. Also to be recommended is the very inspiring, and pleasantly surreal, experience of discussing the logical categories of what must necessarily be, the conceivable and the inconceivable – with a Year 6 class at a village school in Suffolk.

A parallel and very practical aim of these exercises is of course to provide the sense of personal integrity and boundaries that will allow the student to engage antagonists inside and outside of the classroom in a positive and respectful way, without feeling threatened by the opinions they are presented with. **We are not talking about holding one's ground at all costs – we are talking about the ability to consciously choose when and how much to accept or reject of an interlocutor's viewpoints.**

Note that in the structured pair and teamwork debating exercises afforded by Cooperative Learning, the candid

verbalisation of otherwise hidden thought processes gives teachers a unique insight into the assumptions and real-time thought processes of each individual student on which to base follow-up (which in turn creates a truly interactive classroom as the real-time development of meanings paves a more realistic way than any abstract lesson plan).

"Deep thinking" is an endangered species, and never has it been as urgent as it is at the present time to speed its recovery, since children have ready access to and are unavoidably exposed to the conditioning power of an ever expanding cloud of acculturation floating through constantly multiplying combinations of worldwide digital media and peer interaction, that have supplanted and undermined the socially binding processes and narratives that have traditionally operated within the nation state and more specifically, within the geographically localised communities and families in which most people live their everyday lives. The defencelessness of the state in the face of the enveloping transcendency of globalised technique, has destabilised the very ground required for the cultivation of localised narratives and shared values, seriously compromising any sense of certainty with respect to identity – and therefore, with respect to the solidity of subjective reality itself – it is all 'up for grabs'. This vulnerability mirrors the earlier crisis of helplessness of the individual, the family, the tribe, the clan and the entire existential order of the 'ancien regime' in the face of the overwhelming ascendancy of the modern state in the wake of the French Revolution. 'What goes around has come around!'

Returning to the *Trivium*, it is worth quoting Dorothy Sayers at this juncture:

> "Has it ever struck you as odd, or unfortunate, that today, when the proportion of literacy throughout Western Europe is higher than it has ever been, people should have become susceptible to the influence of advertisement and mass propaganda to an extent hitherto unheard of and unimagined? Or ... do you sometimes have an uneasy suspicion that the product of modern educational methods is less good than he or she might be at disentangling fact from opinion and the proven from the plausible?"

"Information wants to be free." No governmental control can stop "radical" or "extremist" ideas from reaching our children – in fact, given the free flow of sewage that is flushing around in the bowels of the worldwide web, Islamists may be the least of our worries – but we can make sure the Trojan horse is dismantled and burned, if not politely rejected at the door. And should the Greeks have something to offer – well, that's at the discretion of a forewarned and fore-armed Trojan Commander-in-Chief to determine.

Coming full circle, it just so happens that grammar, rhetoric and logic (*manṭiq*) formed an integral part of the traditional Islamic madrasa curriculum; so no radical Muslim cleric can object to UK state schooling for implementing them in the curriculum.

THE TRAP

We have collectively wandered into a minefield. But what minefield? The nation-state and the complex set of supranational protocols that have attempted to hold everything together, more often unsuccessfully than otherwise, are clearly over. Ukraine; Syria; Iraq. Even relatively minor instances such as the Scottish referendum and Catalonian autonomy are a symptom of the overall disintegration. All of them together place great strain on a creaking and makeshift experimental apparatus. That is bad enough but when you consider that they are merely the diplomatic and political results of an entire worldview that is in collapse, then you begin to understand the dimensions of the problem.

Mr. Cameron's and Mr. Gove's political forebears of earlier generations were global beings with a wide understanding of disparate societies and cultures. They were men and women whose subjects were ordinary Muslims of diverse cultures, and they knew the Muslims and Islam too well to fall into the kind of hysterical prejudices that their 'heirs' have fallen prey to. Churchill, for one, considered the British Empire to be Muslim because of the great preponderance of Muslims among its peoples without that in any way imperilling 'British values'.

The problem is: how do human beings of different cultural leanings, creeds, ethnicities and languages get on together? It is not merely a British problem. All over the earth, the borders are vanishing, and immigrants and refugees come and go. In Turkey, there are almost five million Crimean Tatars. Over the last century, Turkey took in countless Macedonians, Bosnians, Croatians, Daghestanis and more. Saudi Arabia was until recently an almost automatic destination for the destitute Muslim refugee. And so on.

"The multicultural" has been tried, but when the nation itself is in disarray, how can it work? The American potpourri model has been seriously proposed, but its main failing is that it has to be imposed at the barrel of a gun and over the dead bodies of those it intends to 'accommodate'.

Nothing is made any safer by the concomitant rise and emergence into the foreground of the financial undertow that created the necessary conditions for the whole saga in the first place. And it plays a not inconsiderable part. It has intellectually transformed British society from one predicated on a commitment to public service and indeed, 'noblesse oblige' however imperfectly carried out, into one whose quotidian reality is selfishness. Thus, when the Secretary of State for Education posits British Values, is he citing those of Margaret Thatcher and James Buchanan, the philosopher who derided altruism? It is a very real problem.

Now the Muslims arrive on these shores. The overwhelming majority of them have not come as zealots, but rather as economic migrants determined to make their way in the world and to a very large degree with a fulsome admiration of 'British values' as something advantageous for themselves and for their children. They are, however, somewhat shocked at the signs of decay they have encountered here, both moral and economic, although they have not the historical tools to make proper sense of what they see. They enter their children into the school system determined to get the benefits of a modern technological and scientific education at any cost.

Because of their complete commitment to it, their still undiluted thrift, industry, temperance and an almost abstemious way of life; and because of their determination to see their children succeed, they make a positive mark in these schools. Of course, that is only one side of the story and there are many examples of dysfunctionality and community breakdown, divorce, youth criminality, drug-taking and many more unsavoury outcomes. Nevertheless, many educators have seen large numbers of highly motivated third and fourth generation Pakistani and Indian children. And now, finally, there is also a generation of Muslim educationalists, trained and qualified within the British system.

If there is any truth to the original 'Trojan Horse' missive, and this is by no means certain, then it may indicate the presence of a dangerous kind of hubris and triumphalism on the part of some of these Muslim educationalists. That it should amount to a conspiracy is highly unlikely. Surely, we have moved beyond the paranoia of the *Protocols of the Learned Elders of Zion* type.

But what of the event itself? The reaction of the Secretary of State for Education and Ofsted is an attempt to enframe the situation within the Enlightenment paradigm, being able to count upon a general unawareness of its origins and its nature and, in the process, also an attempt to enframe Islam and Muslims likewise, even though they originate outside of this paradigm. We can see this writ large all over the world although it is certainly not conspiracy. But we see the determination to regard the so-called 'Sunni-Shi'a split' as somehow parallel to the 'Catholic-Protestant' schism, thus indicating the necessity for an 'Islamic Reformation'. This assumption is somewhat hasty for, as Mark Twain observed, "History does not repeat itself, although it does rhyme."

Mr. Gove's attempt to enframe Islam and Muslims within a set of Enlightenment values that are themselves in deep crisis, by calling on 'British values', when the British themselves are flailing around hopelessly as they struggle

to define them, presents a degree of paradox. Values such as binge-drinking? Credit card abuse? Neglect of the elderly and vulnerable? Parliamentary expenses fraud? Total war? Killing peaceful protesters? Police corruption? Rejection of refugees? Institutional racism? Sexual license and promiscuity? Abortion on demand? Assisted suicide? Freedom of speech in the form of ubiquitous hardcore pornography?... What exactly does he mean? Or perhaps it refers to that great cosmopolitanism that made the Empire. Or perhaps not. Let us see...

On Western or British Values

May we set aside the superficial distractions that are offered as reasons for what is beginning to emerge, and ask what the real issues which underlie this scandal are?

The discourse that is being presented for us to believe, the ideological state position, is that the UK is at serious risk of attempts at violent overthrow by hordes of brainwashed fundamentalist extremists, immune to reason and totally opposed to our civilised way of life.

These hordes, some of them as young as two, are currently in British schools where unscrupulous teachers and governors plot incessantly to raise a generation of Islamist Jihadists – at taxpayers' expense! – who will eventually wage war against British civilisation and values in order to establish a medieval code of punishments for anyone who disagrees with them.

In order to prevent this from happening, schools where this brainwashing is already established must be given over to new teams of management, who will undo all of the damage that has been done to young minds and set them on the path to enlightenment values such as freedom

and democracy. Schools which have not yet been inspected will be immediately spot-checked without notice, so as to prevent them from hiding the disgusting practices which they no doubt have been concealing from us up until now. No stone will be left unturned until all Muslim children are safe from the risk of becoming violent extremists.

If this sounds exaggerated, it is not. Teams of inspectors have been sent into kindergartens and found them to be ignoring (deliberately?) the risk of extremism to which these 2-4 years olds are exposed. The message is clear – if nothing is done, we all risk violence from these children when they grow up. Similarly, Michael Gove is on record as believing in the 'conveyor belt' principle – shown to be false in empirical studies – which holds, for no good reason, that a conservative Islam will lead to fundamentalism, then extremism and then violent extremism, if not in all, then in a significant number of cases. Research on who is actually involved in violent extremism shows, on the contrary, that religious conservatism and even fundamentalism and extremism have no causal role. Terrorists may declare that Islamic principles are the motive for their actions, but socio-psychological problems are the underlying cause revealed by scientific studies of the phenomenon. What this means is that we have two sides in these events, both declaring high-level moral principles which they only superficially espouse while the real motivations are only thinly veiled if not out in plain view. Does anyone really believe that Tony Blair declared war on Iraq for humanitarian reasons?

So we might conclude that the war on Muslim majority and Islamic schools is less about a concern for the safety

of children and the general public than it is an expression of plain old racism and xenophobia. If we look at what is actually being said and done regarding this issue, that conclusion is not difficult to come to.

The most obvious feature of the recent and ongoing scandal is that just about everyone involved has no, or very little, personal experience of Muslims, Muslim schools and Muslim communities. It springs from the 'Little Englander – Great Briton' mentality of the generations who now lack the global cosmopolitan experience administration of the Empire once assured although they somehow aspire to that long lost glory. **What is being argued over endlessly is based almost entirely on what people have read in the press or seen on television; it is a media event. This phenomenon was confirmed by research several years ago which revealed that the vast majority of British people had learned almost everything they know about Islam and the Muslims from the infotainment industry – newspapers, magazines and television. Today, this material gets recycled through the blogosphere, producing all manner of mutant hybrids and memes.**

Consequently, the most obvious scandal has been a huge increase in ill-informed and aggressive attacks on Islam and the Muslims of this country. These attacks extend from sly innuendo to thinly veiled calls for ethnic cleansing, with every degree of unpleasantness in between.

This is paradoxical to anyone with half an eye. The main reason given for the avalanche of hatred being poured out on the Muslim communities is that there are fundamentally important values operating in the UK, which Muslims are implacably opposed to and therefore Islam has no future in this country. If, moreover, Muslims try to maintain that Islam is not opposed to 'Western' values then they are either lying or deeply confused about the nature of their own beliefs.

These Western values, which Muslims are supposed to be against, are, among others:
- **Freedom of thought**
- **Respect for others rights**
- **Tolerance of difference**
- **Respect for the Rule of Law**
- **Equality of treatment**
- **Democracy**

Yet what are Muslims being told now? You are free to think what you like as long as you agree with us? Rights only apply to people who agree with us? Diversity does not include being Muslim?

The problem here is that secular liberalism is really rather intolerant of those who refuse to accept it in its entirety, who may have doubts about some of its consequences – such as the abolition of any meaningful religious faith. It is clear that you can be tolerated, respected and given freedom only within the somewhat problematic limits of enlightenment rationalism.

But these are relatively abstract considerations in the current context of calls for the eradication of Islam in the UK. **More seriously, respect for the rule of law rings very hollow in the context of British society today where a thoroughgoing disdain for legality appears to be the order of the day in both the international and domestic spheres** – from assisting in torture and secret rendition to participation in unilateral US wars of aggression and regime change, from bankers to politicians, policemen and journalists, entertainers and educationalists, no sector of society has not recently come under scrutiny for lack of probity amongst some of its leading representatives. If there is a swamp to drain, we don't have to look very far; to single out the Muslim communities is blatant prejudice.

Equality of treatment? If Muslim publications were full of the kind of propaganda against the 'enemy' we find in the mainstream press there would be an outcry. If the comments sections then included the kinds of hatred and calls for violence we find on the internet, endlessly recycled and repeated, new laws would be passed and millions spent on controlling extremism, because it would be (even more) Muslim extremism. **Yet anti-Muslim extremism, or Islamophobia, is now the everyday reality for Muslims and Muslim institutions. The asymmetry is mind-boggling.**

And finally, democracy. **What this word is even supposed to mean is contestable; it is not just a system of government but a code word for the ethos of western-style liberal societies.** Everyone kind of understands what it means more or less. It is about being safe from violence, having a reasonable standard of living and a range of shopping and entertainment options. Once you have that, you cannot really ask for more. **The social institutions that support this comfortable lifestyle include education, health, a working economy, sport and leisure industries, police and judiciary reasonably free from corruption, a free press and a system of representational government.**

So which of these are Muslims supposed to be opposed to?

And, conversely, which of these are immune to critical examination? Frankly, there are problems with all of it and if Muslims have something to say on this score, is that automatically a problem? Let us see...

Question: What is the state? The disturbingly prescient and understandably demonised philosopher Friedrich Nietzsche, rightly took this to be a question worth asking and his reflections are chilling:

> "The state? What is that? Well then! Now open your ears, for now I shall speak to you of the death of peoples. The state is the coldest of all cold monsters. Coldly it lies too; and this lie creeps from its mouth: 'I the state am the people'..."

In the light of this it can hardly be surprising to see, in the current debate concerning British values and identity, how inextricably the state has woven itself into the fabric of the matter. Firstly, we note that the terms of the debate have been dictated by the state itself through its leading ministers, quite literally by way of issuing what can best be understood as a challenge that dares Muslims primarily to expose themselves to the consequences of professing an identity or 'values' that do not expressly and explicitly owe recognition and affirmation to the state, whether in terms of 'nationality', 'citizenship', patriotic allegiance or undying gratitude. This presumption is made possible because we have passively, over the centuries, absorbed the poisonous lie identified by Nietzsche, to the effect that the state and the people are indivisibly one and the same. The well known Muslim intellectual and founder of the Norwich Muslim community, Shaykh Dr. Abdalqadir as-Sufi, demonstrating the grasp for which he is rightly recognised, if not always fully appreciated due to being somewhat ahead of the times, reveals further sinister dimensions to Nietzsche's profound question, which are particularly relevant to our thesis regarding the nature of the state, its trajectory towards tyranny and the very real dangers contained in the profession of or association with anything other than what might be deemed 'British values' (i.e. the values of 'the people'):

> "**The pharaonic [state] model is marked by the deification of creational realities in the triple (Trinitarian) coding 'people=state=leader.' Thus, opposition to any one of the three terms is taken as opposition to the others in the series. That the people cannot be an ontological reality, let alone an existential organism that can be experienced or known in any holistic way, indicates the essentially mystical and religious nature of the doctrine. The first term implies that the collective reality of the social body is in its turn equal to each and every individual member, and so any statement made about the collective reality will be a valid statement on each citizen. It is clear from this that any citizen who should from his own existential reality, whatever its condition, feel forced to question or negate the social project, must be considered deviant and, more drastically, could be defined as a non-person, since he no longer fulfils the required definition of a person, i.e. one who confirms the social project in all its ramifications.**"[3]

Leaving aside the physical elimination of its own citizens by executive order without due judicial process (as in the case

---

[3] *Resurgent Islam* 1400

of US citizen Anwar al-Awlaki who, having taken refuge in the Yemen, was sought out and assassinated by drone strike) we have also recently witnessed the most egregious examples of the state's readiness to consign its own citizens, by bloodless administrative device, to the twilight zone of 'non-person' status: The USA's strategic revocation of the whistleblower Edward Snowden's passport leaving him stranded 'stateless' in the transit zone of a Moscow airport stands out, as does the cynical case of the Australian Wikileaks activist Julian Assange, indefinitely trapped within the Ecuadorian Embassy in London, potentially for life, in the name of justice and the rule of law. The UK's repeated threat to nullify the passports of anyone leaving the country to fight alongside 'jihadists' in Syria or Iraq against the despotic Assad or Al Maliki regimes, respectively; this has been the response of the British state to the repetition of a noble precedent set by tens of thousands of idealistic young citizens from Western democracies (including the UK) who left the peace and safety of their homes to join the International Brigades and risk their lives fighting alongside the Republican forces against General Franco's Nationalist Regime during the Spanish Civil War of the 1930's. Of course, there has never been any denial that their willingness to depart stood for anything more sinister than idealistic political naivety, or anything less than the altruistic expression of the highest of Western values. Today the reward for such 'naivety' or 'altruism', as the case may be, is arrest and/or imprisonment or statelessness. How Western values have progressed! **The awful truth, even in the very midst of the recent self-congratulatory claims being made by government ministers to an impressive list of universally recognised civil aspirations as exclusively 'British values', is that democratic civilisation has** degenerated into unimaginable levels of tyranny and lawlessness as the nation state gives way to the 'world state'. MFAS Chancellor and legalist, Abu Bakr Rieger writing on the subject of Nihilism and Human Rights, draws upon the insights of radically independent and highly regarded Western political philosophers in order to arrive at the following sinister revelations regarding the ultimate trajectory of modern state power:

> "In a seminal work *Homo Sacer: Sovereign Power and Bare Life* written in the late nineties, the philosopher **Giorgio Agamben introduces the concept of the concentration camp into the centre of the political discourse. According to Agamben the goal of modern power-politics is no longer the national, sovereign state but, shockingly, the concentration camp. He portrays the camp as the true symbol of the modern age. The ultimate in world-political sovereignty and power is revealed in the camp, that is, in the decision to strip speech, law and space from 'bare life'. This prophecy is being fulfilled in Guantanamo and in the known and unknown camps of that world state which is emerging today. To Agamben the camp is now an integrated and long-term component of the global nomos. The famous definition of Carl Schmitt regarding political sovereignty, namely, 'Sovereign is the one who decides on the state of emergency' is thus given a terrible extension of meaning: 'Sovereign is also the one who is able to set up a camp.'** [...]
>
> "Let us reflect a moment upon the meaning of the world state, about which Carl Schmitt rendered

another interesting definition. According to him, nihilism is the separation of order from location. In other words, to him the world state is nihilistic as it separates order from location. Or, as the Italian philosopher Antonio Negri defined it in his work *The Empire*: 'The world state is an empire without any recognisable centre.' If we now think of Agamben and Schmitt's insights together, the following remarkable, almost mathematical equation is revealed. Again we take as our point of departure the principle that nihilism is the separation of order and location. The following conclusions may be made about the concept of the 'camp' and the 'state of emergency':

The camp symbolises location without order. It is a bio-political nomos which transforms life into 'bare life'. The state of emergency, on the other hand, symbolises order without location, a nomos devoid of legality and without a centre."[4]

The Collapsing Edifice

As the main title suggests, we are concerned with offering a detached *ex post facto* perspective on the exaggerated and disproportionate public panic that has been triggered by what has turned out to be a hoax letter sent last year to Birmingham City Council warning of an active 'Islamist' plot to take over state schools by infiltrating and 'stacking' their boards of governors. **Whoever engineered the release of this hoax certainly knew which 'buttons' to press in**

---

[4] see MFAS Politics of Power Module lecture 7 'Democracy and the Post-nation State'.

order to detonate the explosion of hysteria and paranoia which, following America's neo-conservative lead, has been stoked to fever pitch as a matter of their extended domestic and foreign policy logic obsessed as it is with national security against the nightmare of Islamic terror and maintaining the heightened atmosphere of fear and imminent danger best understood as the permanent state of emergency that is required to justify the imposition of even the most extreme encroachments upon pre-American civil liberties and principles of justice, whether in terms of almost limitless secret surveillance of its own and the world's citizens, the assassination, secret rendition, torture and imprisonment of its own and the world's citizens without due process or the immunity of its armed forces to prosecution for their criminal behaviour overseas and resort to the judicial transparency of the Star Chamber at home, all in the name of protection against a deadly 'Islamist' threat that there is growing evidence to show is being actively promoted and invented, certainly in the US, by major government security agencies such as the FBI by means of 'profiling', 'entrapment' and what one very comprehensive investigative report by forensic lawyers Downs and Manley[5] has termed 'pre-emptive prosecution':

> "They term the government's approach to Muslim suspects 'pre-emptive prosecution,' defined as 'a law enforcement strategy, adopted after 9/11, to target and prosecute individuals or organizations whose beliefs, ideology, or religious affiliations raise security concerns for the government. The actual criminal

[5] http://www.projectsalam.org/Inventing-Terrorists-study.pdf

charges are pretexts, manufactured by the government to incarcerate the targets for their beliefs.' Just so. Go after Muslim men because, by dint of being Muslims, they might be inclined to become terrorists. Nail them before they have the chance. Downs and Manley found that 289 out of 399 (72.4 percent) of the convictions boasted of by the Justice Department were purely pre-emptive, and another 87 out of 399 (21.8 percent) contained elements of pre-emption, meaning the defendants might have been engaged in 'minor, non-terrorist criminal activity' but the activity was manipulated and inflated by the government to appear to be terroristic."[6]

The whole amounts to a shocking manifestation of the nihilistic chaos and current breakdown of law and order unmistakably evident in the democratic nation state model that results from the separation of order and location, as identified by the legist Carl Schmitt and the logic of the concentration camp revealed by Giorgio Agamben referred to previously.

Therefore, what better pretext than even the vaguest whiff of an 'extremist' plot against one of the state's most formative and crucially important domains to spur into action Theresa May (sensitivity to White House expectations being a prerequisite for the key post of Home Secretary) and Michael Gove (neo-conservative by nature and inclination, following the unbroken recent line of 'special relationship' persuasion from Thatcher and Joseph; to Blair, Mandelson, Blunkett and Clarke; and now we

---

[6] https://web.archive.org/web/20150323083621/https://blog.timesunion.com/carlstrock/inventing-terrorists/467/

have Cameron, Clegg and May)? And what an irresistible prize for the extremist conspirators! **A prize that is much more likely to be seized, if Gove has his way, by privateering corporations, preferably 'shock doctrine' style, in the wake and under cover of some enormous disaster, be it natural or manufactured, after the American charter school model!**

Is it simply the case that **Muslim communities in the West find themselves occupying the ground floor of a collapsing building? As we have seen, the UK is unravelling at the seams as a coherent and viable sovereign entity. Once confidently and assertively situated at the centre of a powerful worldwide empire, it is now stripped down to a small island nation awkwardly displaced off mainland Europe (both physically and politically) and looking with hopeful longing for affirmation and friendship out across the American Sea (or the Atlantic Ocean) for a 'special relationship'. Her inhabitants are now experiencing a crisis of identity, whereas once upon a time they were wont to find it reinforced through instant recognition and positive affirmation on every continent. Now small minded 'English nationalists' such as the EDL (English Defence League) and Britain First complain that the distinct English identity has been subsumed within the British Union as surely as the cross of St. George has been submerged into the 'mishmash' of the 'Union Jack'.** The situation has been made still worse by the political orthodoxy of multiculturalism that has washed in from across the Atlantic with its innovative 'pick 'n mix' of hyphenated-Americans used as a Cold War propaganda 'bag o' tricks' to project an image of American inclusiveness embodying the human diversity of the free world, whose leadership it claimed, in answer to the inviting cosmopolitan outreach of the Marxist International and those who would raise the question of America's shameful and embarrassing civil rights record, Jim Crow segregation laws, lynchings and imprisonment of Blacks (now African-Americans), the rampant discrimination against all visible minorities (Latino-Americans, etc.) and the genocidal mistreatment of the continent's Aboriginal peoples (Native-Americans) in the name of Manifest Destiny (or White Supremacy), while claiming superiority over Soviet communism and any other potential rivals. Hence, it was necessary to convey worldwide the universalism of the American way, whilst at home imposing upon Blacks and other radicalised and dissatisfied minorities, a rationale that would justify the demand for their unquestioned patriotism, rather than be led by the example of Malcolm X, who had begun to look to the Third World for humane support and solidarity, and to the UN (perhaps naively) for legal redress against the US government regarding the open abuse of their human rights, and whose infamously unpatriotic response to the assassination of JFK ("Chickens coming home to roost") resulted in his suspension from his position as leading spokesman for the Nation of Islam. **Though not nearly so acute in the UK, the rationale was analogous. However, in both cases the advent of multiculturalism would provoke a backlash from nationalist elements within the white majority, for whom this multicultural logic was yet one more shroud over the corpse of the historical white British and American WASP preferred self-image. Add to this the world banking crisis of 2008 and the inability of national governments to shield their populations from the resulting economic recession, job losses, evictions** and austerity measures; or from the 'unfair' competition from migrants and refugees for scarce jobs, housing and welfare benefits.

As an exercise in socio-political engineering the technocratically driven project of centralised national government and social organisation on a national scale has continued for some 350 years, having obliterated along the way any surviving traces of prior modalities of societal organisation, identity and governance, substituting any true historical record with a compulsory narrative predicated upon the irresistible logic of a linear evolutionary progression of human civilisation from the cruel darkness of monarchic despotism and feudalism to the sunny uplands of liberal democracy as we know it in the 21st century. **This failing experiment, undertaken in the name of scientific progress was born within the crucible of the so called Age of the Enlightenment and the forces of bloody carnage unleashed by the French Revolutionary call to 'Liberté, Égalité, Fraternité', which resulted in the subsequent template for the modern nation state provided by the Napoleonic dictatorship. What has this to do with Schools in Birmingham? It is relevant because in this modern democratic society in which it has been our collective privilege to be informed and educated, history in any real sense has been all but replaced by an entertaining preoccupation with the narrowly private focus of online family ancestry searches. The serious study of history is also well on the way to extinction in most secondary school and even university courses and curricula; except as a source of dates, soundbites and imagery for the reinforcement of feelings of national** pride and fealty to the state; history has been devalued within the educational system as unlikely to lead to a remunerative career or to make much of a contribution to the economic growth of 'UK plc'. It is important to realise that there is a world of difference between constant exposure to the determined 'presentism' and distraction of breaking news headlines, and exposure to the processes of historically contextualised reflection that might enable us to understand how and why we have arrived at this present juncture and where we are most likely to end up. The prospects are grim.

Apart from what we have already observed regarding the imposition of state structures upon people's natural, traditional or otherwise chosen means of exercising their once free and inalienable right and responsibility to organise themselves, whether it be along tribal, ethnic, religious lines or all combined. Peter Hitchens highlights an interesting case in point in his Mail Online blog:

"Thanks to various treaties between church and state, in which the Churches were in a strong position because of the work they had done, the state conceded large freedoms to the churches, especially the freedom to continue to maintain schools in the state system, which had a religious character and which are allowed to choose many of their pupils on a religious test. **In my view the Church of England were diddled, because the promise they extracted in return for ceding control [to the state] of many schools, that all state schools would have a 'broadly Christian' daily act of worship, and that the national faith would be taught as such in** schools, has been comprehensively broken. I use the word 'comprehensive' deliberately. The creation of vast new American-style high schools has made it far easier for these obligations to be shelved, forgotten or bureaucratically obstructed. 'We just don't have a hall big enough. We can't fit it in to the timetable. We don't have the qualified teachers', etc. I'd be very interested in a survey of how many non-RC state schools actually deal with the Christianity question. I think it would show that most pupils could get through their school careers without ever encountering anything resembling organized Christianity, as a living faith. Now, one of the things I really like about Muslims is that they are not having any of that. They value their faith, they believe in it, and they see it is one of their main duties in life to pass it on, undiluted, to their sons and daughters."[7]

Looked at more closely, it is not really that "the Church of England were diddled", but that the English people, whose Church it was, have been 'diddled' and that this was the general pattern across the board of traditional social institutions, organisations and functions.

The point here is that the Trojan Horse legend is far more persuasive as an analogue for the enforced usurpation of peoples' inherent freedom to take direct responsibility for the independent and autonomous management of their own affairs (including their children's education and upbringing) on a traditional social scale in keeping with their own local and immediate needs and requirements. Instead, however,

[7] 9/6/14 http://hitchensblog.mailonsunday.co.uk/2014/06/the-word-extremism-does-not-mean-anything.html

with the state being in a position to impose its vast defence, education, transport, health and welfare infrastructures upon the population, it has exacted various forms of taxation in exchange for these 'gifts' and in order to pay off the national debts and balance of trade deficits accumulated in our names as collateral. Matters are made worse by the increasingly obvious fact that the vast national scale of social organisation as a technocratically driven experiment over the past three centuries is failing. **The accelerating collapse of the national project under the entropic stresses created by the uncontrollable cyclical financial shocks inherent in the global corporate and banking order we refer to as 'the Markets', and by the supranational imposition by the US, or NATO, or the UN, or the EU, of untenable political, military, financial and logistical pressures.**

In addition to this there is the centrifugal pull away from the centre towards the devolution of powers and calls for regional independence, as evidenced in cases such as the Scottish referendum in the UK, Catalan and Basque separatism in Spain, and the Northern League in Italy, whilst in the Ukraine we can bear witness to the breakup of a nation in the tug of war between the nationalist impulse in the East towards Russia and the 'technically constituted' citizenship of the EU in the West and even as we speak we are treated to the dramatic spectacle of state collapse in Iraq and Libya both defenceless in the face of international intervention. However, within the EU itself, recent national and European parliamentary election results have revealed the tensions between a growing right wing nationalism, which has arisen in countries across Europe in reaction against the perceived advance of EU integration at the expense of national identity and sovereignty, and also point to unprecedented levels of instability and uncertainty regarding the nation state's survival as the key structural component and repository for sovereign legitimacy within the international world order as once understood and accepted throughout the 20th century. **On the basis of the 'last in first out' principle, Muslims are well advised to run the risk of appearing 'unpatriotic' and head for the nearest exit before the whole thing comes down on top of us (we'll be blamed for it anyway!). We must seek refuge in and recover our natural identities as denizens of the world, rather than submitting to the pressures of political correctness and volunteering for 'democratic' toleration, administrative containment and intolerable isolation as suspect 'citizens' within the artificial silos of dangerously unstable and increasingly autocratic nation states be it UK, USA, Russia, Egypt, Ukraine, Syria, Turkey or Iraq.**

Applying the Educational Thought of Shaykh Dr. Abdalqadir as-Sufi[1]

Muhammad Mukhtar Medinilla

وَجَآءَ مِنْ اَقْصَا ٱلْمَدِينَةِ رَجُلٌ يَسْعَىٰ قَالَ يَٰقَوْمِ ٱتَّبِعُوا۟ ٱلْمُرْسَلِينَ ۝ ٱتَّبِعُوا۟ مَن لَّا يَسْـَٔلُكُمْ أَجْرًا وَهُم مُّهْتَدُونَ

A man came running from the far side of the city, saying, 'My people! follow the Messengers! Follow those who do not ask you for any wage and who have received guidance. (Sura Ya Sin: 20-21)

Bismillahir-Rahmanir-Rahim

Last January in Granada, during the VII Educational Seminar, when Uthman Morrison proposed that I might contribute to this course, I expressed my gratitude and delight to be here among you, but also my surprise because, to be honest, I couldn't imagine what I could possibly bring to the table, being fully aware of the level and quality of the people of Norwich and England, regarding the subject of education, and

---

[1] Delivered as a lecture on August 2, 2015 in Ebrahim College, London, and repeated in Granada on August 22, 2015, for the 12th anniversary of the Great Mosque of Granada.

more specifically as it concerns Shaykh Dr. Abdalqadir as-Sufi and his work.

In fact, it caused me a certain feeling of ambivalence; on the one hand, what better theme could I find more amenable to treat with than Shaykh Abdalqadir's thoughts on teaching? I was delighted! But on the other hand, I knew that talking about this subject would be a problem, as I would always feel dissatisfied with the end result. How was I to do proper justice, in a single presentation, to everything we have lived and learned with our Shaykh? However, this feeling of apprehension, was overtaken instead by the desire to embark upon a task that had been in my mind for quite some time; to gather the whole subject into a book. Therefore, preparation for this presentation has served as just the prompt I needed finally, to rise to this challenge, and to fulfil what I regarded as a personal obligation, to leave a record of our lived experience, in relation to his teaching for the coming generations, especially for the benefit of the up and coming teachers, who might find it useful to their development.

Because we have received, both collectively and individually (here I am reminded of so many men and women, and their personal experiences with the Shaykh), an essential heritage that we need to transmit to our young; we embody it, it is all within us. When Shaykh Abdalqadir was going to leave Granada in 1993, he said on our farewell: "When they could have killed me, they didn't do it; now it doesn't matter, because you have it all." The transmission had taken place. We were already a community, like the one described in the *āyah* recited by Sidi Bashir Lund:

وَجَاءَ مِنْ أَقْصَا ٱلْمَدِينَةِ رَجُلٌ يَسْعَىٰ قَالَ يَٰقَوْمِ ٱتَّبِعُوا۟ ٱلْمُرْسَلِينَ ۝ ٱتَّبِعُوا۟ مَن لَّا يَسْـَٔلُكُمْ أَجْرًا وَهُم مُّهْتَدُونَ

> "A man came running from the far side of the city, saying: 'My people! Follow the Messengers! Follow those who do not ask you for any wage and who have received guidance.'"
>
> (Surah Ya-Sin, 20-21)

In everything that has been said so far, throughout this course,[2] there is much of the educational thought of Shaykh Abdalqadir: Uthman Morrison, Idris Mears, Fatima Dennis, Ibrahim Lawson, Abdassamad Clarke, Abdarrazaq Goodall... And I also think about other people who could tell us much. Perhaps, between us all, we will represent the embodiment of everything that has been transmitted by our beloved Shaykh over these last fifty years.

In truth, I regard all of these experiences as my own; all of the educational projects over the years, in the different communities of Shaykh Abdalqadir, on so many levels; from the madrasas, such as the Madrasa of Mallorca and the Madrasa of Larache, to centres of higher education, Dallas College and Lady Aisha College in Cape Town; and also the primary schools, La Maestranza de Granada, among others, and even those who have attempted home schooling, etc., from the first school experiences in Norwich, the forerunner of those which would later follow.

---

2 The module of The Muslim Faculty of Education: "The Question Concerning Education"

But I will take the community which I belong to, the community of Shaykh Abdalqadir in Granada, and the point we are at, as my central theme, because as an educator, I must speak from existential experience, rather than abstract hypotheses, because there is no teaching without a connection to reality. I think this is the best approach. I don't know much about this place [Tower Hamlets], neither its context nor circumstances. I only hope that some of what I say, from the perspective offered by my own physical distance and context, may be of some use.

I have consciously left aside on this occasion, the intellectual speculation and reflection on the subject, which I consider to have been well covered in my talk, entitled "Islamic Education versus Assimilation",[3] in order to offer you, instead, the close and sincere account of a lived experience. It is a risky business, but I think it is essential to examine all of our fine educational concepts, and the extent to which they are being applied or not, in the reality of my community, to remind my people of the great value of what has been transmitted to us, and that there is nothing better than to put it into practice. For, how can we continue to talk about important matters, such as *ijaza*, if we don't first elevate the qualities of trust and honour in our communities? The question of trust in our teachers is still unfinished business for us in Granada.

Whilst acknowledging *The Apprenticeship of Wilhelm Meister*, whose main protagonist provides a central narrative thread for this talk, I would also like to quote another character in this key novel, Yarno: "Man is not happy until he limits his undefined aspirations", in order to bring focus to this presentation. I have

---

[3] p.114

narrowly defined the field, our Granada community, placing limits on the great expectations usually awakened by Shaykh Dr. Abdalqadir as-Sufi's ideas on teaching, in order not to suffer the disappointment of failing to encompass what was anyway beyond my scope, and by limiting myself to what we have experienced. It has been, for me, an opportunity to reflect upon the role and teaching of Shaykh Abdalqadir in our community. It has to do with our 'now', where we are headed, the way forward.

So, let us allow Wilhelm, and perhaps other characters from *The Apprenticeship of Wilhelm Meister*, to accompany us from time to time along the way, given the great importance of this novel for us as educators, Europeans and Muslims, and given the impact it has had upon the thinking of Shaykh Dr. Abdalqadir as-Sufi.

When he was 13 or 14 years old, Shaykh Abdalqadir took "important bearings" from this book. In an excellent piece of work on the book, Ahmad Gross provides us with the following account: "In the middle of WWII his friend's sister [Netta Hannah], a war pilot, was about to die of tuberculosis. He visited her while she was in bed. There were two books beside her. She offered to pass on to him everything she had learned in her life, if he chose the right book. The two books were *The Culture of the Renaissance in Italy*, the most respected and renowned book by the famous Swiss historian Jakob Burkhardt, and *The Apprenticeship of Wilhelm Meister*, in the English translation by Thomas Carlyle. 'I examined them with shaking hands, and chose Goethe. I had made the right choice.'"

Shaykh Abdalqadir's life as a young man, as in Wilhelm's life and as he himself recounts in his autobiography, "had seemed not only without destination, but in itself nothing but a troubled and turbulent wandering." And like Goethe's character, he took the path of theatre. They both did it with a high purpose: Wilhelm, to transform the theatrical institution in the most elevated school of a whole nation; Shaykh Abdalqadir, to resolve the two great questions that would occupy his whole life: the couple, the relationship between man and woman, and the end of the state. From his experience in a theatre company, Wilhelm went on to the great theatre of the world; Shaykh Abdalqadir, to a personal voyage to decode and liberate a world which was in the grip of and enslaved by the structuralism of the modern state and the power of usury.

Shaykh Abdalqadir connected with this intellectual current, which has always been present in Europe and the Western World: Goethe, Schiller, Nietzsche, and Wagner. These men, together with Belloc, Jünger and Heidegger, had completed for him "a whole mosaic of understanding". "These thinkers had pointed the way to a new destination for me and a new beginning." But it was Goethe, in a way, who had opened the door to the threshold of Islam.

How many similarities we find between *The Apprenticeship of Wilhelm Meister* and *The Book of Strangers* by Shaykh Abdalqadir! And how to forget, when thinking about this time in our Shaykh's life, the beginnings of our own journey, as young people, and thus to address the importance – in the words of Hajj Abdallah Luongo, may Allah have mercy on him – of "honouring the highest aspirations of the young people amongst us." "This passing on and transmitting" – to continue with Hajj Abdallah, may Allah have mercy on him – "of whatever it is of understanding Allah has favoured us with is a seminal element in Shaykh Abdalqadir's teaching. The educating of our youth together with the dynamics of an ongoing *da'wa* is the clear affirmation of Allah having honoured us with the highest *deen*, and the only one acceptable to

Him. Wherever this is taking place is where the authentic work of Shaykh Abdalqadir is happening."[4]

"Nobility cannot be transmitted by an institution; this can only be done by a clean society; clean in its streets, clean in its transactions, in all its relations, in every sense." These were the words of Shaykh Abdalqadir in 1990 when we were gathered in the old *zawiya* of San Gregorio, to start the school project. More than twenty years later, in his book *The Interim is Mine*, Shaykh Abdalqadir observed: "The recovery of the human species from its present devolution requires controlled union and guided upbringing. In the case of humans, personal education is, by definition, also social. Not just an educational group but a social nexus is required to fashion humans of quality."

It could be said that the first step, without which an authentic education will not be possible, is the establishment of a community with *amr*, because the recovery of the traditional form of teaching is linked to the recovery of this form of Islamic governance *par excellence*. As Shaykh Abdalqadir says in the preface of his fundamental work *Root Islamic Education*: " ... the true pattern of Islamic society – *emirate* ruling the people and some *fuqaha'* ruling the *amir*, by defining *shari'a* limits, not by cult of personality."

If we begin to talk about education in mere 'pedagogical' terms, we will be blocking real education from taking place, real teaching from being established. When Amir Malik, the amir of our community in Granada, asked Shaykh Abdalqadir a few years ago, to write a 'definitive' book on education, the

---

[4] Abdallah Luongo, "Shaykh Abdalqadir as-Sufi, Leading Intellectual of Our Time," 6th Annual Conference, Islam in Europe, 2009, A Celebration of the Main Mosque of Granada. https://robertluongo.blogspot.com/2009/07/shaykh-dr-abdalqadir-as-sufi-leading_16.html

response of Shaykh Abdalqadir was clear: "But I've already said everything I had to say on education!" And this is true, but his contribution to education has generally been addressed at everything that must be established 'before' we arrive at the field of teaching, and without which it doesn't matter which teaching method we use, as it will not have an effect.

In Granada, the first thing we need to ask ourselves is where we're going as a community, and then consider what educational model can lead us toward that goal. Is this school model appropriate for the direction we need to follow? Will this school serve to form men and women capable of redefining the world in which we live, of firmly establishing our position as Muslims and replacing a logic of madness and disaster with a new way of thinking guided by the honor of Islam?

I know I am touching on a delicate subject, but we cannot pretend to find an educational model in this land if we are not actively working to find an answer to the role of the Muslims in Europe in this time. We are talking about establishing a renewed Islam in Europe, with formal relations among the communities, with local *amirs*; establishing links between them regarding all aspects, including commerce and economy, outside the banking and financial circuit; establishing a post-usury culture; reconciling the native converts with the immigrants, helping those among the latter who are in difficulty, strengthening ties between different Muslim groups. Our presence here today, over and above these words, bears clear testimony to our desire to advance toward our political unity, just as our great spiritual connection already is.

And in my opinion, all Muslim communities should start, in as much as possible, school projects and colleges from school age to the end of high school level. In addition to the attention given to children and the young, these represent an important structuring factor in the communities where they are integrated. The educational question is not 'only' a matter for those who have children; if we frame it in this way, we will be placing the business on a very low plane. These days in England have made me reflect: given the historical moment in which we find ourselves, it might be a blessing for us in Spain not to have the 'facilities' or 'freedoms' that exist here, home schooling, free schools, *Waldorf* schools. In Germany they have thousands of *Waldorf* schools. Are they articulating change, a real transformation of the system? Our 'difficult' situation in Spain forces us to find a solution from the social sphere, to grow as a community.

That afternoon at the *zawiya*, Shaykh Abdalqadir came down from his room, into the *musalla*, where we were gathered, sat with us and said: "In truth, a school is not necessary to be educated, but you really need the school." In a way, he was also telling us: alongside the essential social nexus, you require a team of teachers. The school emerged from the community, promoted by Shaykh Abdalqadir; a task which has always been taken on by the amir with the will to protect Muslim identity and to form our children in a correct manner, with *tawhid*, beyond the state system; a school that would serve as a conveyor belt for the transmission of the teachings of our Shaykh to successive generations. We were all present there: the authority, the amir; the educators, the teachers; and the base of the *jama'at*, the families. That was the framework; those were the necessary elements for the children's school, the great school. What we weren't perhaps aware of at the time were the great challenges that this path held in store for us all.

And all these challenges are still present today. It might seem that, in our history as a community, we have clashed over and over with the problem of the school (and I suppose this to be the case in all those communities that have one); but the school wasn't really the problem. Rather, the school was merely the visible tip of a huge iceberg, the great mass of which lay submerged beneath the surface. The same dynamic is reflected in the state system, under which it is not possible to find a solution to the perennial 'education problem'; they are constantly debating the issue, without realising that their disastrous educational system is only a reflection of the parlous condition of public and private life overall in modern society.

Therefore we find ourselves on an almost head-on collision with these questions that are so sensitive for us, those which Shaykh Abdalqadir had already encountered in his youth, about which he has warned us, giving us specific and general indications, arguing the case and revealing these in almost all his written works: the establishment of a healthy and vital relationship between man and woman, and liberation from the mythic power of the state. These two elements, in the words of Abdussabur Kirke, the "vital stems of his work", were already present as seeds in the work that would emerge from this 22 year old young man, from this Wilhelm/Shaykh Abdalqadir, who revealed in his first theatre plays that these didn't belong to the "enormous accumulated information" of a student, but rather to a perceptive quality which corresponded to "another kind" of teaching. When Abdussabur asked him about this, he replied immediately: "That's it; I knew, but I didn't know I knew."

"Do it! Do it!"

With this indication, which concluded the latest message which Shaykh Abdalqadir sent us early in January this year, during the VII Educational Seminar of the Al-Andalus Educational Foundation in Granada, he called us to form groups of seven, nine or ten men, closely united by a *ruhani* (spiritual) alliance. He called us to establish between us, quoting his own words, "*asabiyya*, a close and sincere brotherhood, based on the blessed *sunna*". Which means, in fact, establishing the highest form of nobility in European history. He sent this message to all the educational projects linked to him, and which had gathered for the seminar.

"Do it!" This is his latest word to us. And I have reflected much about this. A few days later, a group of ten young adults from our community had gathered, ready to "do it", bound by commitment to Amir Malik. And it was by this message from Shaykh Abdalqadir, the inspiration which emerged from the high aspirations of all the projects and, as a final impulse, the words of Abdalhaqq Bewley, which closed the gathering, those which he pronounced at the end, beyond his wonderful speech on education, words which were not written, that just came out of his heart, calling our young to support each other, to work together, to *live* the light emanating from the Messenger of Allah ﷺ and transmitted by our Shaykh. This is the model of Madina Al-Munnawara, our chance to survive in the face of the collapse of the structuralist state system, incapable of educating people. In his own words: "The Shaykh or guide must gather seventy men, like Sayyidina Musa, or ten men, like Rasul ﷺ; these small *jama'ats* will be able to go anywhere and do anything. And they will be the ones who are the guardians of Qur'an and Shahada."[5]

---

[5] Shaykh Dr. Abdalqadir as-Sufi, 2012 Cape Town Moussem talk.

I have asked a few of the members of this group[6] about the nature of what they are doing, about their vision of what they want to achieve, to learn for myself whether they realise the enormous importance of their endeavour. And I have also tried to communicate to them my conviction that this is the mature fruit of more than thirty years of a community's history. Their choice is the fruit of a sowing, on a land fertilised by very specific conditions: three generations, a dynamic amirate and families and individuals who have overcome many trials. Nearly all of them have experienced the school of the community as children, most of them have then been at the madrasa in Mallorca, Dallas College in Scotland, Granada and South Africa, even at the Shaykh's house, and including a wide variety of experiences over time related to our communities around the world.

There is no doubt that we have a generation that has received this transmission. They are young adults, working shoulder to shoulder with their elders. We have an example right here who was a student at our school; we are now working together on the school project to improve what we have today. We don't need to say much to understand each other; sometimes a simple glance will suffice. This he has received from his own experience as a student.

During the great difficulties we have had of late, in which we have taken hard knocks on various fronts, our community has demonstrated its strength, its unity. Suddenly, when we needed it most, during the general 'crisis' meetings, with great temperance, a firmly rooted knowledge surfaced which clarified and readjusted the situation. I felt I was reliving all those moments in which Shaykh Abdalqadir transmitted to us that

---

6 The attendees at the Muslim Faculty of Advanced Studies module on "The Question Concerning Education" in London, May 2015

same teaching. The past, our tradition, returned to illuminate the present. I observed the younger ones amongst us and could perceive how a true recognition, a learning process was taking place. They need the closeness of those men and women who have been immersed in the teaching of our Shaykh. It becomes very necessary to hear the voices of those who treasure this knowledge in our communities.

And I remembered the words of Shaykh Abdalqadir during one of his talks at the old *zawiya*: "The circle of knowledge, of study, of wisdom, all of this transforms man. So we have to recover the strength I had seen in the faces in this community."[7] It was a time in which Shaykh Abdalqadir taught us. The houses were open and we lived according to what he taught us.

Because we have been in serious danger of becoming a community of "home and mosque and forget anything else"; we have been on the brink of turning what was to be a path of liberation into a 'religion'; and we need to understand that to carry on with our lives, with most of our children in state schools, and the little ones in the kindergarten, while the grown-ups are dedicated to earning a living or 'pursuing their dreams', would be a disaster. Integration, contrary to the idea of assimilation, and in a worst-case scenario, a pure case of 'assimilism'[8], means to assume the active, dynamic position of creation and growth, leadership and transformation of a truly Muslim identity.

How often Shaykh Abdalqadir has called us to this understanding! And how often he has called us to establishing the authentic Islamic *milla*, which means to soak up, like a

---

[7] Shaykh Abdalqadir, "Discourse on Muhajirun, Ansar and Nomads"
[8] p.114

garment emerging from dyed water, completely saturated with the practice, the interrelationships and transactions (*mu'amalat*), the behaviour (*'amal*), of the *deen* of Islam!

It is necessary that we watch ourselves constantly, asking ourselves whether we are establishing a society which allows a real transformation of its individuals, or if, on the contrary, we are conforming, accepting limitations, deceiving ourselves with superficially convenient social relationships, rather than real coexistence. It is, in short, a choice between truly 'islamising' ourselves or playing games instead. The position of Shaykh Dr. Abdalqadir as-Sufi lies in the *āyah* in the Generous Book of Allah: "*Say, Allah! And leave them to their games.*" (Qur'an Sura al-An'am 6:91)

What we must understand is that reliance on Allah "is not" – in his own words – "an intellectual belief; this is something that is transmitted and it is also an educational process." How important it is to grasp this! It is connected to upbringing, to the early years, to the family; it is also connected to the school, and encompassing these two spaces, the community, which strongly defines both.

This is the reason why Shaykh Abdalqadir has always placed great importance on upbringing, our care for the complete development of the child. In his talk "Iman and Education", given in Klöntal, Switzerland, in 1990, he said: "I am proposing a view of transformation of yourself that involves the responsibility of the transformation of your children. Or, to use a Goethean expression; to allow your children to emerge."

Twenty-five years later, these words still resonate in our homes, but it is plain to see that in the following generation, the key generation, there are young adults with small children, where problems are arising, situations that were suffered by their parents are being repeated, situations against which we had fought for decades. And, as usual, this ends up being reflected in the children, in their development and in their conduct, as consequence of the conflict between men and women. We have been a community with too many divorces. And we have been witness to how Shaykh Abdalqadir suffered because of this. When he still lived with us, one afternoon after the recitation of the *Wird*, having heard about a recent divorce involving people he really loved, he said, clearly distressed: "It is not character, it is not character! Those who divorce after living together for years, it's not an incompatibility in their characters! It's an economic matter!"

In April 2006, in Cape Town, after a night of *dhikr*, Shaykh Abdalqadir gave a *dars*, a reminder for the communities of Granada and Cape Town – "The Responsibility of the Fuqara", which I would have liked to read in full, because it is well worth it, but don't worry, I will limit myself to a few excerpts:

> " ... the politics of the Muslim community is not run by the 'ulama or *fuqaha*, it is run by Leadership. But, ... everything that is done must be founded on '*ilm*, on the knowledge of these rightly guided '*alims* who protect the Book of Allah and the Sunna of Rasul ﷺ.
>
> " ... Inside the household the finance must be according to the Shari'at. The use of the money and the spending of the money and the responsibilities to wives and children must be correct – not what suits people but what they are ordered to do by Rasul ﷺ. Then they must see that the children are educated properly. They must see that the children are taken from this culture of the streets and protected from the streets.

" ... What has happened to the children? What are they doing? What are they wearing? What company are they keeping? ... You must be concerned for your children, and concerned for their education and you must also understand what Shaykh Muhammad al-Kasbi said in his *khutba* (at the opening of the mosque in Cape Town), which is that if you are with the *jama'at* you are safe ... You cannot shut yourself up in your house. You cannot shut yourself up out of the way of the community. You must take your responsibility. Your responsibility is to see that the *Deen* is taught."

When La Maestranza de Granada school started in 1990, Shaykh Abdalqadir gave three words of advice to the families, and we understand that these were associated with, and complemented the teaching work:

Husband and wife must not argue in front of the children or in a place where they can be heard by them.

Man and woman must have separate bedrooms.

To perform the *salat* together and to be led by the head of the house; the man is the *imam* and he must perform all the *salats* in the central area of the house.

Shaykh Abdalqadir coined the phrase "the collaborative couple", "moved" – as he said himself – "by what Allah says in the Qur'an about the people who will enter the Garden: '*They will enter alone and in couples.*'" On one occasion, Shaykh Abdalqadir asked a man: "What do you want to do?" The man answered. Then he asked his wife: "And you? What do you want to do?" She started saying, "Well... I want to continue studying..." but she stopped herself suddenly, and then continued: "But before anything, to follow my husband." Shaykh Abdalqadir shouted:

Subhanallah! and he sprang off his chair and said: "That's it! That's it! ... This is the sickness of Granada: to believe that man and woman can go in different directions." After a moment of reflection he added: "Man and woman are for each other like a refuge in the storm."

In *Fantasia of the Unconscious*, D. H. Lawrence says: "You've got to fight to make a woman believe in you as a real man, a pioneer. No man is a man unless to his woman he is a pioneer ... But no man ever had a wife unless he served a great predominant purpose." And Shaykh Abdalqadir transmitted to us: "Every man of this community must be a leader of Islam and say, 'We are going to do this in our time!' ... You must say, 'This is where we are going. This is what we want to do,' then the woman must help. Without the support of the woman, nothing can be achieved." ("The Responsibility of the Fuqara").

Shaykh Abdalqadir has always called us to abandon the family project and the search for provision, to establish justice, to understand that man in this time has been degraded. In "Iman and Education" he says:

> "... we must take the Nietzschean image of reaching the Übermensch as an Islamic duty, an Islamic call. The Daʻwa of Islam is to call people to be more than they have been. As Nietzsche indicated, you cannot just suddenly have an *Overman*, you have to create a bridge to an *Overman* by saying, 'The way we are is not enough, we have been downgraded, so we must consciously transform ourselves. ... At the moment it is only possible with an élite group of people who have the courage to begin the procedures of your re-education.'"

And he has always called us to leave the house, to 'de-domesticate', to unite with other men, to sit with them and not to fight them, to lay matters on the table and reach agreements. On more than one occasion he has recalled this *hadith* of the Prophet Muhammad ﷺ: "The Muslims are like two hands washing," adding later: "How can two hands wash each other if they don't come together?"

Shaykh Abdalqadir continues: "People of conscience must educate themselves. And this transformation implies being demonstratively educational towards the new generation"; but "unless you completely transform the process of your life, it will not have an effect." And this requires a profound understanding of the time we are living in.

Then there is fear, a fear I can perceive in our community, especially among the young, a fear in the face of the responsibility of becoming leaders, because this is the rank of those who take on this task. Wilhelm, in *The Apprenticeship of Wilhelm Meister*, reflects upon *Hamlet*. Hamlet knows that in order to have justice, a heroic act is required, and he knows it is possible to achieve this through a heroic act; but he is hesitant concerning whether he will be capable of taking it on or not.

However, no one should lag behind, because if they do, they will turn their family into their *raison d'être*, and the first victims of this will be their children. I remember Shaykh Abdalqadir at the old *zawiya* in the Albaicín encouraging us: "Make mistakes! Make mistakes!" That is what I would say to our young, over and over: "Don't be afraid! Make mistakes! Make mistakes!" At times, they seem to be like modern day Telemachuses, searching the horizon for a sign of their fathers. What are they looking for? I ask myself. Is there anything that the fathers haven't yet given their sons? Were they absent, lost at sea, amidst the storms? The truth is that so long as Telemachus fails to recognise Ulysses, his position, his behaviour cannot be manly, but rather, passive in the face of the suitors' abuses.

And they shouldn't make the mistake of looking back to settle the score, rather, they must look forward to the moment of reconciliation, as Wilhelm did when he finally confronted his father's legacy (the bourgeois model). To recognise it, to take it, and from it and through it, – in the words of Abdalbasir Ojembarrena – "to discover the sacred duty of serving with nobility."

They must not be Telemachuses, crouching under the shadow of their fathers and, therefore, incapable of acting like men; nor Oedipuses, wishing to kill the father and, in consequence, waiting for the ideal that never arrives, idealists, 'waiting for Godot'. It is necessary that they go beyond this and understand that they must be themselves, because Ulysses had already left his message. He was king of Ithaca! And our young men must become aware of this: the message has been delivered; they have all the necessary elements.

How important this is: identifying with the father, the transmission of masculinity and all its associated values. It is not an invention that, statistically, there is a relationship between problematic boys and the absence of male models in the family, because they are physically absent or simply disassociated from their children's education.

Intergenerational harmony is essential, because the key to cohesion is in avoiding an existential void between one generation and the next. It is necessary to see that the existential necessity of our young to find meaning in their lives is being satisfied. Because it can be particularly difficult for them if, having grown up with a fractured heart, they might feel suspended 'between two cultures' and they don't know exactly where they are.

Shaykh Abdalqadir associates "the creation of a community (*jama'at*)", the "basis of a post-statist society" with the necessary establishment – in his own words – of "a new educational method which preserves the spontaneity of the young for their entire lives,"[9] because social and individual change are not possible separately; both transformations must necessarily run together.

This is our challenge: to create spontaneous men and loving and conscious women, as Shaykh Abdalqadir defines them in *The Ten Symphonies of Gorka König*.

And I have made reference almost exclusively to the men because they confront the most difficulty. It is true that it's harder for women to survive in a system mostly built by men, but men have the added difficulty of recovering their masculinity, their manhood, and being in reality. And 'a man' is not made. Men are made!

But you have to be aware of this. As Abdallah Luongo, may Allah have mercy on him, says: "Together with this desire (an essential element to take on this heroic task), the other key element is that we must have – from when we were in our early childhood – been loved." There is an undeniable link between the yearning for transformation in the young man and the love he received in his first years, and a profound attention.

How great has always been Shaykh Abdalqadir's concern for the care, protection and education of the very young. And how many times he has warned us – as in "Iman and Education" – that 'the wound of children comes from the home', and has called us to realise that what happens in our homes is decisive.

---

[9] "The Collaborative Couple" see p.137

On one occasion, at the beginning, when the school was in his *zawiya*, and I worked upstairs, where his home was, in one of the rooms he had lent to us to be used as a classroom, he knocked on the door and he asked me very kindly to leave (something he did once in a while). He entered and sat with the young ones for a good while. That evening, after reciting the Wird, he addressed everyone, angrily, because he had found out that the parents didn't talk to their children at meal times. He said: "Only so-and-so has a good cultural level and has an interest and knows about many things. This is because they talk at the table and his father tells him things."

He himself is an example of the power of the family. At the beginning of his journey, his life's journey, of what seemed the chaos of his life, the strong family imprint, and his family history, which cannot be separated, produced in him "flashes of meaning" that indicated in the odyssey of his existence "that there was meaning to be found and that illumination" – in his own words – "would one day emblazon both the road and the landscape."

We are talking about elements that are necessary for the transmission of trust in Allah to take place. Trust is also educated. In his work *The Ten Symphonies of Gorka König*, Shaykh Abdalqadir notes: "The creation of a new élite is not merely a pedagogic problem; ... for no school can produce an educated youth unless the infantile and formative pattern of the self has been consciously modelled to break the biological imprinting that produces robotic repetition of the parental crime."

Our community in Granada finds itself at the crucial point of being able to understand this, to understand that a cultivated society is a renewed society. The Shaykh has told us over and over that "Islam is not a culture, Islam is a filter for all cultures;

a sieve through which the culture passes and leaves behind any unhealthy elements." A crucible, which separates the essence, the gold, from the impurities. As Shaykh Abdalhaqq Bewley has told us, it is part of our mission to reach "an expression of Islam that will transcend and transform the classical tradition of Greece and the European tradition."[10]

"We have everything we need in our own tradition."[11]

Our Amir, Malik Abdarrahman, has established a library, at his *diwan*, to which we all have access. He has a yearning, which you cannot help but admire, to raise his education. He asked for advice from Abdalbasir Ojembarrena in Cape Town; He asked him to provide him with a list of all the works that he recommended he should know. And he set out. Every time you visit his rooms, you find new titles.

I remember the words of Shaykh Abdalqadir many years ago, in the old *zawiya*: "There is nothing in the libraries... but everything is there." In that context, those words referred to a rejection of a bookish knowledge, disconnected from life and action. But today, the Amir has understood, and he's an example for all of us, the necessity to form oneself, to elevate oneself, to achieve a perfect balance – as Goethe shows us in *Wilhelm Meister* – between thought and action. He periodically invites groups of men, from both generations, to his *diwan*, to hold discussions that stimulate intellectual work and reflection, over what is learnt in relation to our lives, and the situation of the community.

---

[10] Shaykh Abdalhaqq Bewley, *Root Islamic Re-education*, Granada, 2014. See p.1 of this book.

[11] Ian Dallas, *The Ten Symphonies of Gorka König*

In general, there is a process of *paideia/Bildung* taking place among us; a yearning for true education is awakening. A few years ago, during the annual education seminar, when we talked about *paideia*, *Bildung* and other terms that belong to our Western culture, to many of our people thought it was like "double Dutch." Today, alhamdulillah!, *paideia* is a reality among us. Because the decisive factor in all *paideia* is energy, and energy is emerging.

Heidegger translated *paideia* as *Bildung* (not forgetting that it was Goethe who introduced the 'Theory of Bildung' in a decisive way). *Paideia* is a *Bildung* (formation/education) that concerns the very essence of our souls, the foundation of the human condition. And the essence of *paideia* is not to 'pour knowledge' into an 'unprepared soul'. True *paideia* captures and transforms the soul to make it apt to the perception of things as they are.

We therefore identify ourselves with *paideia*, in the sense of a mode of educational activity which aims for the individual to become virtuous, to reach *areté* – nobility, *futuwwa* – and incorporates an ethical dimension in his relations with others; along with an identification of politics with education, in a manner that *paideia* gives access to *politeia*, which is to know how to co-exist. *Paideia* has its roots in the community. And educating for the community doesn't mean to hand down an external will to the young ones, be it from the state or any other form of indoctrination (as is the case with many so-called 'Islamic' schools), but rather to awaken a clear understanding of the human relationships they will experience. *Paideia* brings a live and active spiritual vision and a community of destiny, the Muslim communities as the new polis; the polis which orders and distributes individuals and their functions around the model of the *'amal* of Madinah al-Munawwara. This is the great qualitative leap that must happen in Europe: from the Muslim associations, which offer 'assistance', to communities with *amr*, which imprint 'existence'.

And we identify with *Bildung* in the sense of an integral formation of the individual according to a model of man that is above the limitations of the power of the state. *Bildung* represents the opposite of the basic European model of the Enlightenment and the French Revolution: national, state education.

But all this is only possible if we establish among us an impeccable *adab*. And I'm not referring to greeting each other, offering up our seats and all the forms of courtesy among Muslims, which must of course be observed, but rather to be capable of recognising each other; in the words of Shaykh Abdalqadir, "giving everyone their due and recognising who everybody is"[12]; that each and every man and woman in this community is able to play their part to their full satisfaction.

A new *nomos*, a renewed *paideia*, a new order requires a new educational model. And this model cannot be apart from the feeling and purpose of a community. And as a community we must have a vision and, in consequence, a direction; and I would go further: a mission, in the sense of a common plan.

Our role in Europe today is crucial. We are a bridge. We are – as Abu Bakr Rieger once said, referring to the Dallas College – "the centre-point where both axes meet." He was referring to our Islamic tradition and our cultural tradition based on Greco-Roman civilisation and the European sciences and philosophy. At the meeting in Meknes of Shaykh Dr. Abdalqadir as-Sufi with his master, Shaykh Muhammad ibn al-Habib ﷺ, as Abdalhaqq Bewley recounted to us, a great meeting took place

---

[12] Shaykh Dr. Abdalqadir as-Sufi, *Commentaries*.

between the Muslim tradition, completely unpolluted by any kind of modernist influence (Shaykh Muhammad ibn al-Habib), and someone who had deeply questioned the modernist values in which he had been educated throughout his life. Shaykh Abdalqadir was the ideal person to receive the pure teaching of the *deen*, the whole transmission that goes back to our beloved Prophet ﷺ and which unifies that which is highest in both traditions, representing Islam the culmination of Western civilisation.

And by Allah, we have been the beneficiaries, in the words of Shaykh Abdalhaqq, of his "renewed ability to authentically understand it (the Tawhid) opened up by the recent discoveries about the true nature of matter and the human being",[13] and, we could add, to understand the language and the form in which we must communicate this in our time and place.

But we also represent a bridge between spirituality and European intellectual thought and its interrupted history (even though there always existed an intellectual current, of free men and women, flowing underneath the surface, to which our Shaykh was connected) for more than two hundred years.

Goethe left his novel, *The Apprenticeship of Wilhelm Meister*, as if it was a treasure, without fanfare, serenely, while the world was collapsing around him and the great values were debunked, severed (as the heads that fell in the squares of the new Republic), for a people who would come to unearth it in the future. "I find," Shaykh Abdalqadir wrote, "*Wilhelm Meister* a radical text,"[14] 'radical' in the sense of 'essential', 'primordial'.

---

[13] Shaykh Abdalhaqq Bewley, *Root Islamic Re-education*, Granada, 2014

[14] Ian Dallas, *The Ten Symphonies of Gorka König*

And it is important to highlight that we are referring to two traditions, but only one teaching. Nietzsche said: "Some people don't find their hearts until they lose their heads." And Shaykh Abdalqadir has said: "When we prostrate, our heart is above our head." Referring to Shaykh Muhammad ibn al-Habib ﷺ and to Schiller, Shaykh Abdalqadir writes: " ... these two great men both saw that there was an element in the human being which was in itself a faculty, and that this faculty allowed a knowledge which was not ratiocination, which was not a logic operation, not a language operation. It was a perceptive experience."[15]

What is necessary is to understand that knowledge will not come back except as *will to power*. It has been taken from us; you cannot have it if you don't fight for it. This is our challenge, our opportunity and a very important part of our *da'wa*. To show, by our example, that it is possible to articulate Power and Knowledge, in harmony.

And this has been the history of our school, the history of a struggle, a struggle, in addition, against the tide of the teaching system in power, and a struggle against our own resistance and scepticism. But Shaykh Abdalqadir defined it clearly: "Do not fall into scepticism! Scepticism is fear!" And he gave us a methodology: two phases; first, the science, to do what is in our hands, rationally; then, knowing that 'we can't do it' and going into the next stage, the moment Allah loves and is expecting, that we turn to Him, glorious and exalted is He, that we ask Him and place ourselves in His hands. Then, Allah gives it to us. Sometimes the thing didn't work out and, as Shaykh Abdalqadir warned us: "It is because you think you can do it

---

[15] Shaykh Dr. Abdalqadir as-Sufi, *Schiller's View of Destiny – A Sufic Perspective*

by your own efforts, instead of asking Allah." And we have witnessed, by Allah, up until today, that this is the case, that miracles exist.

Over twenty-five years our school has had as its main goal that which Shaykh Abdalqadir established from the first day: "The first purpose of the school is to protect the hearts of the children, that they don't break, that there may not be two hearts inside the same chest."

In a succinct manner, these are the principles that have guided the school:

A return to the traditional view of existence, based on Divine Revelation (*tawhid*), in the diverse sciences, activities, and elements that constitute the school. A school where none of its components are in conflict with the others, but rather everything has its place in proper balance, in its right measure and coherently.

To recover the foundation of traditional education, direct transmission, face to face between teacher and student, establishing a personal relationship of trust, respect and affection (love). As Shaykh Abdalqadir has expressed it: "To sit in front of the teacher, knees touching."

The shaping of character. From its beginnings until today, the school has had the *hadith* of the Prophet Muhammad ﷺ as its motto: **"I have only been sent to perfect good character – *Innamā buʻithtu li-utammima makārima-l-akhlāq*'** (Al-Bukhari and Ibn Hanbal); understanding that this *makārim al-akhlāq* of the Rasul ﷺ means, in the words of Shaykh Abdalqadir, "that the Muslim becomes someone who, in the life process, improves himself all the time, all the time, all the time … It is a striving, a reaching beyond, a self-transformation – it is Futuwwa."[16]

---

[16] Shaykh Abdalqadir, *Book of ʻAmal*

The prospect of improvement. That everyone can reach their goals and that, by Allah, you can overcome all the limitations acquired in your childhood and the obstacles that you may encounter. And this is based on the teaching of Shaykh Abdalqadir, as he said: "You may have had a father with kidney problems, a coward, a hysterical mother, both full of faults, and a life burdened with the worst conditions. But know that you can change, that you can reach the top! The heart is the most powerful magnet there is and it attracts everything you place in it."

The education of a new generation that not only confirms the irreplaceable identity of each individual, but also forges groups of young people, united by strong ties of affection, mutual help and a sharing of high expectations and aspirations; a group that is responsible and conscious of their belonging to a privileged generation, which is of enormous significance at this historical juncture.

The pride in being Muslim. The proper satisfaction that is born out of lending value to everything that is related to Islam and the Muslims. The wish to be acceptable to and to belong to the camp of the believers.

An integral experience of the *deen* at school, based on learning without compulsion the basic pillars, according to age and circumstances (Islam); the trust and non-conflictual acceptance of authority (Iman); and excellence in the making and internalisation of *futuwwa*, of the basic norms of chivalry (Ihsan). The coherence between the teaching of Qur'an and the various subjects that are studied at the school must be absolute.

The assumption of our European cultural tradition and the capacity, through this tradition and its language, to understand the meaning of Islam – because Islam is, without a doubt, its culmination.

The object of the school is Truth. And the teacher-student relationship is a transaction, a transfer of energy and knowledge. We both walk the same vital path, in company and mutual encouragement. We live and learn together. And the connection of what has been learned by the teacher, through his own history, and the learning of the student through his own life experiences, is essential; the value of imitation as the medium of transmission *par excellence*.

Before I continue, I would like to point out that, throughout all these years, we have tried to reach the best equilibrium between the two aspects that constitute education, and that are usually found to be incompatible within the system, separated by a false dialectic between the traditional school, *educare*, 'what comes from the teacher, from the guide', and the new or modern school, *educere*, 'what must emerge from the pupil'. What we have experienced is that these two processes are in fact unified and that they reinforce each other.

This is the same process that occurs between Shaykh Abdalqadir and us, his *fuqara*. We define our teaching as a 'master's teaching', but what happens is that there is a meeting point, between that which we are called to by our guide, and that which wants to emerge from us, as it is well reflected in the famous sentence of Lao-Tse: "Educating is not about filling a void, but rather lighting a latent fire."

And the main characteristics of its methodology are:

A holistic education, and with this I mean to say the orchestrated home-school-community work to encourage complete growth; but also, following Shaykh Abdalqadir's indication, that each person should strive to advance every day in five aspects: the intellectual (starting by protecting the intellect from rubbish), the physical (physical health and vigour), the spiritual (*'ibada*), behaviour (*adab*) and courage (bravery).

A personalised education, attending to each child in his or her vital development. Great importance of tutorship on the teaching level as well as the personal and familiar levels.

For life. Teaching must be education and education cannot become obsolete.

Flexibility of groups. Small groups encompassing diverse ages, and the possibility of establishing all kinds of necessary groupings depending on common interest, levels, etc.

Active school. Working from centres of interest (based on Decroly) that run for as long as they hold the children's interest. Fields of interest (and projects) that encompass all (Primary) schoolwork and which emanate from lived experience and direct contact with nature.

The importance given to the development of language in all its forms. The use of an integral system of literacy.

The school as a place of expression (in all fields: artistic, dramatic, literary, etc.)

The recovery of the natural rhythms of growth, without pressure.

The value given to a good time-space orientation.

Stimulation of the interests and curiosity of the child.

The satisfaction of the needs and aspirations of the children, who learn through enjoyment.

The promotion of one's talents; encouraging and collaborating with the families to support them.

The children enjoy great freedom in the working methods and the diversity of possibilities they are offered.

Not to base the work on textbooks, rather the students make their own books, based on their own experiences and discoveries, taking elements from a great variety of resources.

The imprint of this school has been fundamental for a whole generation who are mostly now married adults today and, gradually, by age group, it has continued on to their younger siblings and their children, until today. Its influence has been important, even on those children in the community who never attended the school. A few days ago I received a heart-warming email from a young woman who was thanking me for that 'something' (that's how she put it) that her generation had received. And she was never part of the school. In truth, they all speak of that 'something' that we perceive intuitively, but we do not know how to give it an exact name.

What I do know is that we have always tried to take ownership, as far as we are able, of a quality we recognise and admire in Shaykh Abdalqadir. It is reflected in this fragment of *Wilhelm Meister* in which Teresa talks to Wilhelm about one of the qualities of Natalia, his future wife: "Yes, she has, like you, the noble searching and striving for what is better, whereby we of ourselves produce the good which we imagine we find. ... When we take people merely as they are, we make them worse; when we treat them as if they were what they should be, we improve them as far as they can be improved."

We currently have a programme of seminars and regular training meetings for teachers as well as those in the Granada community who have an interest in educational matters. This last year we have been working on *The Apprenticeship of Wilhelm*

Meister. In it we will continue to work on the essential aspects of the Muslim educator's training in our time, and in our school, both the small school that is currently functioning, and the future project of a major school. And, gradually, we will also delve into the teaching methods that we think can be useful, starting with Montessori and continuing with the Waldorf curriculum and others.

We will conclude with a brief reference to the school project we are working on, which we have provisionally named *The School of the Shaykh*, and for which we have already found wonderful grounds, on the shores of an artificial lake near the city of Granada, donated by His Majesty Muhammad VI of Morocco.

The basis of this school is essentially what I have explained so far. Up until today, our method has been changing, quite naturally improving as we acquire more knowledge. Concerning this experience there was a crucial meeting in Cape Town, in Autumn 2012, between Shaykh Abdalqadir and the school team led by Amir Malik, in which the Shaykh gave us a number of directives "if we wanted to make it 'his' school." We took these indications eagerly, as our greatest wish was to make it a school that is worthy of the elevated teaching he has transmitted to us. We also remain in direct communication with him, at all times, presenting him with our plans, progress and activity reports. And it is obvious that this connection has lent a renewed strength and dynamism to the whole team.

In the three years since that meeting, we have been developing these elements (which would again require a whole presentation) from different perspectives: from the curriculum and teaching (goals, plans of study, methodology, school organisation, etc.) to its architectural form, as well as the tremendous fundraising work undertaken over these years.

Please allow me to conclude with an account of the last time I saw Shaykh Abdalqadir in person, which revived all those other moments in which I have been blessed with his teaching. He dismissed all of the ground plans we had drawn up (more than three years work!). Nothing was ambitious enough for him; the library, the sports fields, it was all too small. By Allah, three years later, we had a wonderful piece of land, much more fitting than the one we presented to him at that meeting! And it was all by our following of his indications. This is teaching! This is the educational thought of Shaykh Abdalqadir as-Sufi! Aspiring to the best for the Muslims.

That morning he also talked to us about the prefects of Ancient Rome and how we must take inspiration from the British system of Public Schools. "In a society there are people who watch out for each other. Ten houses, ten prefects, and one of them is the head prefect. The boys choose their prefects in an organic manner, the best loved," he told us. Then he observed: "The critique is that this is too hierarchical. That is how they have eliminated authority among the students." And then he pronounced that "the traditional school is a threat to capitalism."

A moment later he said: "The *kafir* system of boys and girls together is the first step toward the destruction of the human being. The Aspen model in the US is a *kafir* model. ... The world of the girls is in the house or within a school organised and led by women, separated from the boys' school." And he emphasised that this is not the men's business, but the women's business.

Another time he turned to me and told me: "The two tasks of the educator are: forming the character and fixing what is broken," and after a second, he added, lowering his voice – "at home." And after a further brief pause: "The teacher must learn from his own history. We must learn from the mistakes of the past to make the mistakes of the present."

"The Amir must be rich and have lots of time, so that he can attend to people, who are not fearful of him as if he were a Caesar. The teacher must be poor and keep very busy," he declared.

A school which is not "Islamic" at all in the modern sense of the term, but rather one that "is in the world", he said later. "You mustn't teach Arabic. The kids will learn it like everyone else, at home, in the mosque..." And he told us how Imam al-Ghazali, even back then, considered it a tragedy that when he visited a village, he would find ten *'ulama* and only one doctor. "What you must detect at the school, however, is who among them aspires to be *'ulama* and then send them to Morocco, Meknes or Fez, to centres of learning where they can train."

For a long time we were set on the idea that the school must have 'everything' (in an attempt to integrate everything that in our current situation seemed disintegrated); but this indication from Shaykh Abdalqadir made us reflect and realise that the best possible holistic education is that each element of society fulfils its function within the overall unity, and follows a common model and goal.

He exhorted us not to pay attention to the political system... "Neither Spain nor the United States," he exclaimed, "only the correct relations between Muslims."

"In Pakistan there are still men," he said later. And he continued: "The language of the Muslims is Urdu. 40% of the students must be from India, Pakistan and Bangladesh, and they must communicate in English. English is the dominant language at the school."

He also emphasised sports, to which we must give great importance within the school. "They must have their minds occupied with the practice of rugby and cricket, abandoning soccer." And he added: "Spain is enslaved by soccer."

"The goal is to form people who can run a country… Our work is to make men. It is the group in the cave, who can then go out into the city and change it… with silver money." And finally: "If all of this happens, I will go to Granada," which for us means that we would have reached our maximum level.

Abdallah Luongo, may Allah have mercy on him, wrote: "It is then a way of being that embodies a way of looking at the world that Shaykh Abdalqadir is able to open for us. Importantly, the Shaykh is not a door or passage but a guide who indicates a way that we can take, as much as we are ready to take it, to reach for our highest possibility."

I have quoted different people because, what I have learnt from Shaykh Abdalqadir has often reached me through the men and women who have followed him. On the Dhikr night of a Moussem of Shaykh Abdalqadir, Shaykh Abdalhaqq in his discourse said:

> "The fruits of the teaching of Shaykh Abdalqadir are manifest in many forms and throughout numerous places on Earth … but the most real and evident results are the men and women of noble *futuwwa* and coherence, of fecundity in their discourse and their example. This was the legacy of the Messenger of Allah ﷺ; it wasn't palaces or artefacts, it was men and women who illuminated the world."[17]

---

[17] Abdalhasib Castiñeira, "Pearls of the Moussem of Sheikh Dr. Abdalqadir as-Sufi," Cape Town, October 2013

One afternoon, when the school was in full swing in Granada, shortly after it began, and we were all involved in a thousand matters that had to be resolved, and the first frustrations were being felt, I was sitting in the *musalla* of the *zawiya*, involved in one of the problems that had emerged, explaining things and even tolerating some bad manners, Shaykh Abdalqadir was observing from the garden outside. And he said to someone who is very close to me: "Why does he stand for all this?" What is important here is that he was aware of the person. It is as if he wanted me to see that there are no schools without educators, and that people are above the project. And throughout time, mostly through other people, he would send me messages that contained a liberating lesson, always exhorting me to reach for balance, to expand my breast and not be inhibited, to free myself from the Christian burden I carried, to lean towards a Dionysian mode and leave my Apollonian nature, and not to become 'Nietzsche's donkey', carrying a burden that didn't belong to me, to "fill my jug" so that I could then pour into others, doing what I liked most and felt most passionate about, even if no one understood; to kick out modesty and throw it down the stairs..., literally using many of his words.

"The only Islamic matter is my life, our life," he said in a discourse, "... we must find the way to deal with life, with freedom, this quality of *fitra* which is not being constrained inside."[18]

His life reminds me of the Prophet Ibrahim ﷺ, because he was young in his youth and he is young in his old age; he hasn't lost his strength, his passion, his *joie de vivre*! This is one of his most important lessons, his continuous example, his being in constant change and openness to the world, to life.

---

[18] Shaykh Abdalqadir, "Muhajir, Ansar, Nomads"

At the beginning of Book Eight of *The Apprenticeship of Wilhelm Meister*, his newly found son, Felix, plays in the garden, where Wilhelm follows him with joy. "The delights of nature were a new spectacle for Felix and his father didn't much know the things that the child was incessantly asking about … On that day, the happiest of his life, it seemed to him that his learning had begun because, on being required to teach, he felt the need to learn."